WHEN REASONING NO LONGER WORKS

A Practical Guide for Caregivers Dealing with Dementia & Alzheimer's Care

ANGEL SMITS, BS, GERONTOLOGY

BARKER
MEDIA

ACKNOWLEDGMENTS

No book comes to be without the help of numerous people. I can't imagine trying to take on something like this without a huge support network of family, friends, experts and colleagues. You've all been so wonderful and important to my work here.

Judy Carlson, Janet Kolb, Lydell Martinez, Jeanne McIntire, Karen Underwood, and Jude Willhoff who encouraged me to take on this journey.

Skee Hipszky of El Paso County Search and Rescue, David Husted of the Colorado Springs Police Department, and Dr. Randall Bjork. Your professionalism and knowledge enhanced mine.

Of course my awesome family, Ron, Jennifer, and Joe.

And lastly, this book is dedicated to the people who

really did the teaching . . . Bess, Sophie, Ike, James, Laverne, Flossie, Dick, Lillian . . . the endless list of people who struggled with their illness and yet gave me more than I could have ever given them.

Thank you.

FOREWORD

It is not often that a clinical neurologist is asked to write a foreword to a book. There may be a reason for that; however, I will seize this opportunity anyway because I was so moved by the way this particular book addresses a human condition which is present in almost every community in the world. Ms. Smits's book is a practical approach for the day-to-day care of the Alzheimer patient.

It has been shown that centenarians have the plaques and tangles in their brain tissue which characterize the senile dementia of the Alzheimer type; therefore, we might think of dementia as an inescapable inevitability if one lives long enough. Ms. Smits has explored many of the issues which accompany dementia. The most troublesome of these are the disruptive behaviors which test the resourcefulness of families.

The format of the book lends itself to reference

use and I would expect that some pages, with the helpful hints listed, will be quite well-worn, indeed. For example, if a family is able to identify situations which trigger catastrophic responses, these troublesome and potentially volatile episodes may be avoided without tranquilizing medications.

We have no cure for dementia of the Alzheimer type; instead, we must provide the proper environment for the patient affected by this degenerative condition. Providing for the comfort, hygiene, dignity, and safety of these patients should be of paramount importance. Ms. Smits's book shows how to accomplish these goals of care.

Although our current dementia care resources are being taxed to a great extent, simply because of the sheer number of people who are demented, there is certainly help for the future if we have an enlightened attitude about caring for our vulnerable elderly. It is my sincere hope that this guide will find its way into each and every home affected by this progressive condition which robs the intellect and memory of the individual affected. Bear in mind, however, that the essence of the demented person remains and provides the key to individualizing care of these fascinating people.

Randall J. Bjork, MD
Colorado Springs, Colorado

INTRODUCTION

If you're holding this book in your hands and turning pages, odds are someone you know is suffering from the effects of dementia. It doesn't matter what name we give its cause: Alzheimer's Disease, Mild Cognitive Impairment, Multi-Infarct Dementia . . . the list goes on and on . . . In the end, the person we know and love isn't the same, leaving us in a position of wanting and needing to help them.

But how do we do that when this behavior and the changes are like nothing we've ever experienced before? This book is designed to help you do just that.

While the cause may be different for each person, the resulting situations are similar. Human behavior is human behavior. The trick is to understand it and use educated guesses and our own humanness to try to engineer a manageable outcome. It sounds more complicated than it is.

I've designed this book in three parts. The first part is the fictionalized story of Rose and Lou. They are not real people, but a compilation of people I've assisted in twenty years of working with the dementia population. The second part is an explanation of what's happening in the journey Rose and Lou . . . and many other dementia patients . . . are traveling. The final section consists of bulleted lists. These lists are by no means exhaustive, but are some of the "tricks" I've learned over the years, tips I've gathered from other family and professional caregivers along the way.

I hope that you'll find the stories as informational as the explanations of what's happening. And the lists I designed to be a springboard for not only your actions, but your thought processes. Don't just try these suggestions verbatim. Adjust them, add to them. Learn not just what to do, but the process of creating your own solutions and success.

Angel Smits
Gerontologist

CHAPTER 1
WHAT IS DEMENTIA?

Rose and her husband Lou bought their small home just after they married. They'd planned to move to a bigger place when they got the money, but they never quite saved enough. They started and raised a family here. When the last kid went off to college, Rose and Lou found the small house was actually the right size for just the two of them.

Rose was happy with her life, content with her three children, two grandchildren, and recent retirement from the school district where she'd taught fourth grade. Two of her kids lived in town, the other only a three-hour drive away.

She relished the chance to sleep in, go on an occasional shopping trip with her daughter, and putter in her garden.

Rose loved to garden. This year, she planned to order lots of seeds. The catalogs were already coming in the mail. She'd spent hours planning, to the point of drawing the garden out on paper. Every time she looked at it, she smiled. It also reminded her she needed to place those orders.

Three catalogs lay spread on the desk in the den. Their bright, pretty pages tempted her to touch and dream. If only they were planted already.

She picked up the phone, dialed the 800 number and pulled her credit card from her purse. A little thrill of excitement went up her spine. The operator answered, taking all her information down—name, address. Funny how numbers kept running away from her. She had to turn the magazine over. She laughed it off. "Must be getting old." The operator chuckled along with her.

The woman thanked Rose very warmly for her order, and Rose smiled. Such a friendly young woman, not something you saw often these days. Rose picked up the next catalog.

Hmm, it looked vaguely familiar. So did the other one. Which number had she just called?

"I should have written it down," she mumbled. Reaching into the desk drawer, she pulled out a pen. This time she wouldn't forget.

She picked up the next book and dialed the 800 number. Weren't these free lines just wonderful? A cheery voice came on the line. She gave her name.

"Oh, Mrs. Davis, is there a problem with the order you just placed? Did you want to add more?" the woman asked.

Something, fear maybe, shuddered through Rose.

"N—no, I'm sorry. I must have dialed the wrong number." When she hung up, she smiled to herself, and decided that's what had happened. She put a big "X" in the corner of the catalog. There. Now she'd remember who she'd called.

She picked up the next catalog and dialed another number. This time a man answered. He took her order with the same friendly manner. She remembered to put the big "X" on the cover.

The door slammed. Lou was home. Lou wasn't retired yet, and worked for a meat packing plant downtown. He intended to work a couple of more years, to add to their nest egg.

Rose always enjoyed the end of each day. They'd share their day's experience over dinner. She couldn't remember what she'd planned for dinner, but knew it would come to her as soon as she went into the kitchen.

Lou smiled at her as he came into the kitchen, a box under one arm. His lunch pail dangled from his other hand.

"Looks like your seeds came." He extended the box to her.

A frown settled across Rose's brow. "What seeds? I was just getting ready to order them when you came in."

Lou's frown reflected hers. He set his lunch pail and the box on the table. This was the third time this week she'd forgotten something major. Monday, she'd handed him his lunch, telling him she hoped he'd enjoy the meatloaf sandwich. At lunch, he'd been surprised to find the box full of Friday's leftovers—no meatloaf sandwich in sight. Yesterday, she'd forgotten he was coming home for lunch. That wasn't so bad, since he didn't always call, but he found her ironing the vinyl tablecloth. He shuddered to think what would have happened if he hadn't come home.

"Rose, are you feeling okay?" He moved over to her. "How did you sleep last night?" He remembered several years ago when insomnia had plagued her. She'd been confused then from lack of sleep.

"I'm fine, Lou." She glared at him. "Why wouldn't I be?"

Lou braced himself for her anger. "You just seem to be forgetting things a lot lately."

"Oh, a few things. Who doesn't?" She turned away from him, pulling a frying pan from the drawer beneath the stove. It smacked against the burner with a loud clatter. "Do you think I'm stupid or something?"

Lou stared at her. He was tired and didn't want to argue with Rose. They never fought much, and when they did, he was usually the one to give in first. He didn't like seeing her angry, and did everything he could to make her smile again.

"No, I'm just worried about you." He heard the fear in his voice and cringed, hoping Rose hadn't noticed.

Rose stared at the pan, frowning. Lou watched panic race across her face and his heart sank. He gently laid a hand on her arm. "How's about I take my pretty lady out to dinner?"

Rose smiled as relief replaced the panic on her face. It was the fourth time they'd gone out to eat in a week.

"Oh, that would be a nice change."

Lou grabbed her jacket from the closet and helped her slip it on, afraid if he let her out of his sight, she'd forget they were going.

The next day, Lou took his eldest daughter aside and told her about Rose's recent bouts of forgetfulness. It was wearing him out, and Melody had always been a big help.

"Dad, you have to get her to the doctor."

"She doesn't want to go." Lou paced away, looking out on the backyard where Rose and their granddaughter, Joy, planted seeds in the garden.

"Do you want me to try and persuade her to go?"

Lou never shirked his duties, but this was one time he was at his wits' end. Admitting that might be the only way to help Rose.

Tears stung his eyes as he watched Rose and Joy laugh. Today, Rose was her usual self, but most of the time he felt as if she was slipping away from him. He missed her, missed talking to her, hearing her opinions, even debating with her.

Over the next few days, Melody had little luck getting her mother to a doctor. It was three weeks before Rose agreed, and then only after Melody lied about the reason.

Before Rose saw the doctor, Melody met with him to explain the situation. "I know there are confidentiality issues, but we're concerned about Mom's memory. I told her it was time for her Pap test just to get her here."

"What have you noticed?" The doctor pulled out a pad of paper and started taking notes while Melody talked.

She told him about the incident with the seeds. She repeated what her father said about Rose getting up in the middle of the night to fix breakfast.

"Does she lose things frequently?"

"Heavens, yes. She's always been a little forgetful, but I found the roaster pan in the bathroom closet last week."

The doctor nodded and made more notes. "Does she have any language problems?"

Melody's hopes rose. It sounded as if the doctor knew what was wrong. "Yes. She mixes up simple words. Yesterday, she called the phone a plant. It started with the same letter, I suppose. Do you know what's wrong?"

"I have an idea, but we need to run some tests. She has some classic symptoms of dementia, but we won't know if it's reversible without the tests."

"Okay," she answered slowly, letting the doctor's words sink in. "What's our first step?"

Over the next few weeks, the doctor ran numerous tests: blood tests, CT scans, and MRIs. Every test they'd invented, Lou was sure. Most of the time, Rose cooperated if Melody went with her. She resisted Lou's help, which took a tiny piece of his heart away each time. He was used to taking care of Rose.

She was up more at night, and he asked the girl across the street, who was out of school for the summer, to keep an eye on Rose during the day. He came home every day and fixed their lunch.

The doctor's office called, and Lou and Melody arranged to meet him. He specifically asked that Rose not come with them, if that were possible. Lou asked the girl across the street to come sit with Rose. He told Rose the girl needed a babysitter.

"We've run every test we can think of," the doctor said, walking around the desk to lean against the front. "I'm afraid Rose has Alzheimer's disease."

Melody reached out and took her father's hand. "Is . . . Is there a cure?"

The doctor shook his head. "There are several drugs to help slow the progress and make it easier on all of you, but there's no cure yet."

Silence hung heavy in the room.

"What do we do?" Lou had never felt so lost. He knew about Alzheimer's. A buddy from down at the plant had told him about it, about having to put his mother in a home.

The tears Lou had held back for the past weeks clouded his eyes. He'd never cried in front of the kids before. Heck, the only time he'd cried in front of

Rose had been when his parents had died. This hurt more than that.

Melody slipped into his arms, and he gave her what he had left of his strength. He had to be strong for her, for the others. He'd always been the strong one.

With a packet of brochures and information about the disease clutched in his hand, Lou headed home. He had a lot to think about, things to talk about with Rose. The doctor encouraged him to tell her what she could understand. He also encouraged him to talk to her about legal matters, power of attorney, and final wishes. He talked about making plans for the future. But . . . what future?

Rose and the neighbor girl sat on the front porch playing jacks. He remembered Rose being the champ when they were in grade school all those years ago. He smiled, and she turned and grinned at him.

His pretty bride. Lord, how he loved her. The neighbor girl headed home, and Lou took her place on the step. He took Rose's hand in his and pulled her close. It felt good to hold her, to know she was still here with him.

"I love you," she whispered and leaned her head on his shoulder.

"I love you, too," he answered, letting the joy of the moment settle over him. He had a lot to learn, a lot to do, but right now he just wanted to enjoy having her with him. He'd make the most of the time they had left. He had to. It was all he had. He pulled her close, kissing her sweetly, tasting the kiss that he'd taken for granted for a long time. Too long.

Rose wasn't gone yet, and he'd do everything in his power to keep her here with him as long as possible.

WHAT IS THIS "DISEASE" CALLED DEMENTIA?

Receiving a diagnosis of any kind of dementia can be a scary—as much because of the known as the unknown.

Dementia is an umbrella term. Like a thief, it sneaks in, stealing memories and, eventually, life. It begins with a forgotten phone number or missed appointment, then moves on to complicate simple actions, making even tying shoes impossible. Finally, it settles in close, making everyday tasks beyond our ability. We depend on others to do what we once took for granted.

This is dementia.

It is defined by Webster's as simply *a condition of deteriorating mentality*. The causes of dementia are varied. Some are reversible, some are permanent and most are progressive.

Reversible dementias are those which can be "cured." Common causes are malnutrition, dehydration, drug interactions and reactions, and such temporary conditions as delirium or a urinary tract infection. With a doctor's care and appropriate treatment, these symptoms usually go away.

The permanent and progressive dementias are not so easily defeated.

There are numerous types of permanent dementia. They include Vascular Dementia (sometimes called Multi-Infarct Dementia), Lewy Body Disease, Mild Cognitive Impairment, Dementia in Parkinson's disease, and Frontotemporal Dementia.

Alzheimer's disease (AD) is the most common cause of progressive dementia, accounting for 50–90 percent of all dementia diagnoses. Recent studies, however, suggest the prevalence will lower with better differentiation and documentation of other dementias.

Alzheimer's is currently the fourth leading cause of death in adults following heart disease, cancer and stroke. It is *not* a normal part of aging. There is an underlying, sometimes medically treatable cause. Despite the fact that the majority of those afflicted are over the age of sixty-five, there may be a reason which can be addressed or changed.

According to the Alzheimer's Association there are 5.4 million Americans diagnosed with Alzheimer's disease. Approximately 500,000 cases are diagnosed each year, and numbers are expected to grow as the population ages. The first baby boomers reached age sixty-five in the year 2010, which account for eighteen percent of the total population. By the middle of this century, the number of Alzheimer's cases will triple.

While America ages, the chance of getting dementia increases. Of people aged sixty-five to seventy-four, three percent have AD. One in five aged seventy-five to eighty-four is afflicted, and almost half of those over the age of eighty-five have the disease. The eighty-five plus age group is currently the fastest growing portion of the U.S. population.

This isn't just a problem in the United States. Other industrialized nations are also feeling the brunt of an aging population and growing numbers of dementia patients.

The need to understand dementia, and deal with it effectively, is ever increasing.

But how does the average person deal with such a devastating illness? We can't go back to school to get a medical degree. Well, we could, but that's not realistic for most of us. We depend upon the experts to teach us. The experts being doctors, researchers, and professional caregivers.

The problem is that the experts are often as stumped as we are. Dr. Alois Alzheimer first identified Alzheimer's disease back in 1906. Since that time, researchers have tried to figure out what causes it, where it comes from, and how to stop it. The research budget for the United States in 2016 was $936 million. While we've made advances, many questions remain unanswered.

Dementia care is expensive. The present national

annual cost of caring for these people is slightly over $236 billion, making dementia care the most expensive disease in America today.

Special Care Units exist in many nursing homes, assisted living facilities, and adult day care programs. Usually, though, this specialized care is more expensive than normal nursing home or home care. The healthcare system tries to cope, but it, too, is overwhelmed, and will continue to be swamped with the numbers growing as they are. Many of these facilities are booked and have waiting lists.

Insurance companies, Medicare, and Medicaid provide some of these care dollars, but the brunt of these expenses falls to families. It comes out of nest eggs and pockets that never prepared for this type of expense.

An overworked medical system means fewer professional care providers, fewer trained personnel, and more dependence on families to fill the gaps. In 2015, unpaid caregivers, usually friends and family, provided 18.1 billion hours of care—care that would have cost $221.3 billion.

Recent studies show that the *annual* cost of caring for a dementia patient with mild symptoms is $18,408; moderate symptoms $30,096, and severe $36,132. Alzheimer's disease, as well as many other of the progressive dementia-causing illnesses can last three to twenty years. The total average cost of care for an Alzheimer's patient from diagnosis to death is $174,000.

This money goes for diagnoses, medical bills, home care, and nursing home care. More of the burden will fall to families, a burden they already shoulder even from the beginning. Seventy-five percent of dementia patients are cared for in their homes, and those caregivers are overwhelmingly women (three out of four).

How many wives go through life keeping track of their husband's socks? It becomes a habit they stop even thinking about. Other tasks come along and are incorporated into the daily routine. They may not even notice the load growing.

Dementia impacts every aspect of life. Early victims manage to keep many of their social skills intact. Some maintain those skills until the end. They can greet people and discuss their past with what appears to be confidence and security. The front is exactly that. A front. A front that strangers haven't a clue is there. A front that only those of us in daily, frequent contact with them see, one we are hesitant to tear down for fear it may be the last thing we have left of who they used to be.

Caring for someone can be a wearisome task for anyone. Pair that with the fact that many caregivers are elderly themselves, or have full-time jobs and other family members to care for, and you have a situation fraught with disaster.

Additionally, there is probably only a few years' difference between spouses providing care for one another. Children is a relative term. A seventy-year-old's "kids" are in their forties and fifties. A ninety to one-hundred-year-old has grandchildren that age.

The fact that many causes of dementia begin slowly means that one person may not even realize they have taken on extra duties. Reality hits when illness strikes and suddenly the caregiver feels swamped.

Caregivers face their own health problems, often exacerbated by the stress of providing for someone else. When that caregiver has to step back, and a different person steps in, the loss of the familiar caregiver only adds to a dementia patient's confusion.

So what do we do? One of the best solutions is to teach caregivers how to care for themselves, and then give them the skills that professionals use in their care roles. Additionally, we can turn to the community and educate them on how to support the caregiver, and how to fill in for them when needed. They, too, need to know the skills taught in the following pages.

HOW THE BRAIN WORKS

First, we need to realize that we can't understand the disease without understanding how the brain is supposed to work in the first place.

The nervous system has often been called the body's electrical wiring. That's a good comparison, but isn't quite accurate. Nerve cells do pass messages similar to that sent along an electrical wire, but the difference is those nerve cells don't actually touch. As shown in Figure 1-1, the area between cells is called a synapse, and the message must jump from one cell to the other across this synapse.

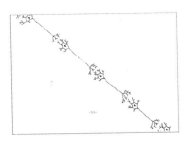

Figure 1-1, Human Nerve Cells

It's like those slates children used to have with the plastic sheet and pencil. You write a message on the board and the plastic sticks to the backing. After you've finished with the message, you lift the plastic and the message vanishes, usually with a loud ripping sound.

A synapse, as shown in Figure 1-1, works in a similar manner (without the loud ripping sound, of course.) The message is written by one cell to another on the "slate" or the chemical synapse between cells. The chemical that receives the message is called acetylcholine. Once the message has been passed, the enzyme with the job to "clean" the synapse (cholinesterase) comes in and "lifts the plastic," erasing the message, making the synapse clean and ready for the next message.

The brain does this hundreds, thousands, even millions of times in a day. It sends messages from "breathe" to "don't touch that" in order to keep our brain and body alive.

The problem arises when dementia enters the brain.

In Alzheimer's disease, the question, "which comes first, the chicken or the egg?" comes to mind. Which occurs first—too much acetylcholine or too little cholinesterase? That's another question researchers are focusing on.

With too much acetylcholine, the cholinesterase can't erase the whole message. That may explain why Alzheimer's patients often exhibit repetitive behaviors. The message keeps getting sent as the brain tries to clear the synapse. And no message to confirm its arrival can get through. With too much cholinesterase, the message is wiped away before it can be sent, perhaps even before it can even be "written."

In Alzheimer's disease, the area of the brain first affected is called the hippocampus, which is located deep in the brain. This is where memories and emotions are housed. That's why an early Alzheimer's patient begins to lose recent memories and can be very emotional.

Next, the disease focuses on the cerebral cortex,

as shown in Figure 1-2, where language and reasoning are located. Often, the early signs are changes in ability to use words correctly, and in using good judgment.

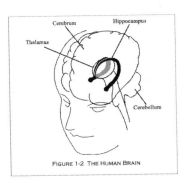

FIGURE 1-2 THE HUMAN BRAIN

Pair that with the frustrations of forgetfulness, and their brain is more susceptible to a stronger reaction. Emotional outbursts and behaviors appear and become more frequent as the disease progresses.

This can be distressing for the patient as well as for their loved ones who may be hurt, emotionally and physically, by the outbursts.

A study done in 1997 by Dr. Barry Reisburg at New York University found that Alzheimer's patients lose abilities in much the same manner that they originally learned them as a child. Like a film rewinding, they retreat through a lifetime of memories—returning to childhood, but not to being a child. They lose their inhibitions and learned behaviors in a backward pattern.

Understanding this progression can help caregivers know what to expect. Professional caregivers have used the Global Deterioration Scale (see Appendix A) for years to help predict functioning and place patients in appropriate care. Family caregivers should also be aware of this scale. Those families who have used it find it comforting and useful in their own process of dealing with the disease.

Though Dr. Alzheimer identified the physiological changes specific to this disease, they're not new; they have been around since the beginning of mankind. What made the changes more obvious was the fact that people live longer now days. There are more people with the disease than ever before.

One of Dr. Alzheimer's patients— a fifty-six-year-old woman—exhibited the signs and symptoms of senility, a condition reserved for the elderly. Dr. Alzheimer noted the formation of what he called plaques and tangles in her autopsied brain.

Plaques are insoluble (solid) deposits of a protein called beta-amyloid and cellular material that collect around nerve cells. Tangles are insoluble fibers of a protein called tau that somehow become twisted inside the nerve cells. Subsequent brain studies have turned up those same plaques and tangles in the autopsied brains of other "senile" patients.

But where do these plaques and tangles come from? How do they get there? No one knows for sure, though there are several theories. Researchers are currently trying to answer that question. Genetic research is focusing on chromosomes twenty one, fourteen, and nineteen, which are believed to be involved in AD, but nothing concrete has been found yet.

There are numerous other causes of dementia which are not nearly as prevalent, but which are just as detrimental to the victim.

Vascular dementia is not necessarily a degenerative cause of dementia,, but it is a permanent one. It is simply, small strokes in the brain, a stroke being when a portion of the brain is deprived of blood and oxygen which kills or damages the deprived cells.

Lewy Body Disease (DLB) is degenerative and is very similar to Alzheimer's in that it affects the chemicals in the synapse. There are fewer of the tangles, but the same plaques. The differentiation is crucial due to the possibilities of treatments available for DLB. Often, DLB is associated with Dementia in Parkinson's disease.

Pick's disease, Frontotemporal Dementia, Creutzfeldt-Jakob disease . . . the list of dementia-causing diseases is many and varied.

Theories and varied diagnoses aside, the reality is that the brain cells die, and the plaques and tangles form. But since, as in the case of Alzheimer's disease, they can't be seen until after the patient has died and an autopsy is performed, how do we diagnose it?

Diagnosis of AD is made through a process of elimination. In all cases, the process is similar. A physician will ask the affected person and their family to describe what's happening. The doctor will do a complete medical history. Frequently, doctors will use a tool called the Mini-Mental State Examination (see Appendix B). This brief test has been used over the past thirty years and asks a variety of questions.

Next, he will order tests. These tests include a complete blood count (CBC) to check for chemical imbalances and deficiencies. A blood chemistry panel will check kidney and thyroid functioning. Tests for illnesses like HIV and syphilis, which can mimic dementia, will be performed. A lumbar puncture may be performed to obtain cerebrospinal fluid. This test checks for meningitis and encephalitis. An electroen-cephalogram (EEG) will check for disease like Creutzfeldt-Jakob. A computed tomography (CT) scan and/or a magnetic resonance imaging (MRI) will be done to look for brain tumors, stroke, and other conditions that affect the physical functioning of the brain.

This may seem like a lot of testing—and for things people are positive they don't have. But as mentioned previously, diagnosis is done through a process of elimination. Not everyone will have every test, but elimination can only be made with the tests' completion.

There's nothing wrong with needing and wanting to know what these tests and diseases are. Learn to ask questions throughout this process. At this point, caregivers might want to invest in a good medical dictionary.

In addition to tests for physical problems, the

physician also conducts a structured interview with the patient. Often, a neurologist or neuropsychologist will be called in to administer this test. The interview will assess cognitive competence. They can estimate the mental competence or level of dementia this way.

Environmental factors and reversible situations are considered, such as nutritional deficiencies, medication interactions, infections, metabolic disorders, depression, head trauma, cerebrovascular disease, brain tumors, subdural hematoma, and hydrocephalus so they can be ruled out and the physician can make a diagnosis of dementia. Other diseases such as Multi-Infarct Dementia, Parkinson's disease, Lewy Body Disease, Pick's disease, Huntington's disease, and Progressive Aphasia can all cause Alzheimer's-like symptoms and can be treated.

After all the tests are complete and the data collected, the doctor makes a diagnosis. Many medical charts use the diagnosis of Senile Dementia Alzheimer's Type (SDAT). Few people actually carry the diagnosis of Alzheimer's disease without some "disclaimer." Diagnosis is not a hundred percent until an autopsy is performed, though doctors are getting better at their educated guesses, and are accurate about ninety percent of the time.

So, we have a diagnosis at this point. What does it mean?

AFTER DIAGNOSIS

When the brain malfunctions, it affects all three major areas of normal brain function: the ability of nerve cells to communicate with each other; metabolism, the way in which the brain uses energy; and the repair of injured nerve cells. All these go into the survival of the nerve cell and ultimately the survival of the entire human body. When they no longer function properly, the whole body suffers.

Now, this is a simplified explanation of a complicated process. The point here is not to study the diseases, but to understand what is happening so we can understand the end result and learn to deal with it.

As mentioned before, we all have this same process of messages being written and erased occurring in our brains constantly. In the AD patient and some other progressive dementias, for a while, the brain compensates by finding alternate pathways— jumping to the cell next door, skipping a damaged cell. Even as the damage progresses, the brain fights to compensate.

Eventually, the brain becomes too damaged. There are few or no alternate routes left. The messages of memory and survival fail to get through. The brain itself may atrophy (shrink) and excess chemicals break down and build up around cells.

Most of the current medications being used for AD deal with the chemical reaction between acetylcholine and cholinesterase. They increase or decrease the balance of one or the other. Unfortunately, they are only effective for short periods of time and simply slow the process. They don't stop or cure it. No one knows if the imbalance causes the disease, or is caused by the disease.

Either way, what happens in a brain with dementia is a physical problem over which the patient has no control. They aren't conscious of what's happening, except to know something's wrong.

Research is constant, trying to find treatments and cures. The more we know, the better prepared we are, and the safer the treatments are for the patients. But caregivers worry more about what's going to happen now. The long road to a cure may be too far away.

Just as it sneaks in to the mind, dementia spreads insidiously throughout society. We can't escape it, but knowing it's there makes it a visible enemy—a companion we can learn to deal with. There *are* answers. There *are* solutions. And in time, there will be medical treatments and, hopefully, cures.

Until then, the need for management of the behaviors by other than chemical means is important. While the cause of dementia varies, the behaviors that result are similar. Professional caregivers have been working with dementia patients and have learned the value of psycho-social interventions. Those interventions, and the processes to create them, are shared in the pages ahead.

CHAPTER 2
CATASTROPHIC REACTIONS AND
THE MYTH OF VIOLENCE

Lou crawled out of bed and headed for the bathroom to shower, shave, and complete his routine as he'd done for the past fifty odd years. Rose was awake, and he kissed her before starting the day. Just like he had for as long as they'd been married.

When he came out of the bathroom, she finished pulling up the bedspread on the bed. He frowned. She wore a simple white shirt and blue pants. The outfit looked nice on her, but it was the same one she'd worn yesterday. And the day before that. He knew she hadn't showered, and he noticed there was a stain on the hem beneath her left arm.

Rose had always been particular about her appearance and he debated about saying anything. Maybe she forgot she'd worn it yesterday. He decided she hadn't noticed the stain and would appreciate his help.

"Rose, why don't you wear something else today?" He tried to soften his criticism with a smile.

She stopped in mid-fluff of the pillow and stared at him. "Why?"

"You've worn that outfit three days now. It needs to be washed and you need to take a shower." There he'd said it. He felt the blush rise in his neck, and reached up to pull at his shirt collar.

"I have not."

"Yes, you have."

"No, I haven't. I'd remember something simple like that." He saw the fear in her eyes that she might have forgotten.

"Not necessarily." He carefully took two steps toward her. "Remember the visit with the doctor? We talked about your memory problems." He didn't use the "A" word, Alzheimer's, on purpose. Not only could he not seem to say it, but the thought of it made his throat close up. He knew how much it scared her. It sounded so . . . so . . . awful. In fact, it scared him, too.

Instead, he reached into the closet and pulled out another pair of pants and a blouse. "Here, I like these."

"No," she growled and wrapped her arms around herself as if afraid he'd take the clothes off of her.

"Rose, stop it," he commanded in a voice he hadn't used since the kids had lived at home.

"I hate that outfit." She glared at him. "I hate you."

"No, you don't." Despite his belief that she didn't really hate him, it hurt when she said it. "Come on." He stepped closer, extending the new outfit. "You'll look pretty in this."

Suddenly, she pulled her arm back, and surprised him when she hit him.

It didn't hurt—much. He was more startled then injured. He dropped the clothes as she quickly scurried away. He heard the bathroom door slam shut and the lock click. The sounds of loud, gut-wrenching sobs echoed off the still-damp tile.

Lou stood there, not sure what to do, or say, or think. In all the years of their marriage, she had never hit him. He'd never hit her. They'd respected each other.

Had he said something wrong? Said it the wrong way? He hadn't meant to insult her. He knew how she liked to look nice.

Throughout the day at work, Lou's guilt grew. He'd hurt her feelings when he insulted her clothing choice, telling her she didn't look good. Slamming his lunchbox onto the table in the breakroom, he let out a heavy sigh. It felt like when they were first married and were still trying to feel their way around in the relationship. Only this time, he wasn't sure he'd ever figure it out—or if he did, that it would work the next day.

He pulled out his cell phone. He wasn't supposed to carry it—company rules—but he'd explained the situation to his supervisor. As long as he kept it in his pocket on vibrate, it was okay.

He dialed the house and sweat broke out on his forehead when Rose didn't answer until the fourth ring. He knew he worried too much, but he felt a bit —no, a lot—off-kilter these days.

"Hello?" Rose sounded in a good mood.

"Hey, hon. How are you doing?"

She was silent a long minute. "Fine. What's the matter?" Fear tinged her voice.

"Nothing. I'm at lunch and thought I'd call you."

"Oh."

Should he ask her about her clothes? Should he apologize? How much did she remember of this morning? Probably enough that if he mentioned anything, she'd get angry again. But what if she was wearing the same clothes, and what if she wore them again tomorrow? He suddenly felt trapped and wished he hadn't called her. He chose an easy tack. What are you doing today?"

"Cleaning house. Nothing any more exciting than any other day."

"Yeah, sounds like work."

She laughed. "Guess we're stuck in a rut."

"That's an understatement," he whispered.

"What?"

"Oh, nothing. I need to get back to work. Just wanted to see how you're doing."

"I'm fine, dear. See you tonight. 'Bye."

"'Bye." Lou disconnected the signal and stared at

the phone. He felt like crap. He'd wanted to apologize for hurting her feelings, but didn't she owe him an apology for hitting him? He slipped the phone back into his pocket and flipped open his lunch box. Nothing looked appetizing. He wasn't hungry.

Maybe he'd go outside and get some fresh air instead.

———

YOU DON'T NEED TO BE AFRAID OF THE PEOPLE IN your care. Being afraid of them takes away your control of the situation.

There are techniques and skills which can, and should be learned by all caregivers to maintain that control. In this chapter, we'll address those specific to the time of the catastrophic reaction and to identify the triggers which spark them. In subsequent chapters, you'll find tips specific to each identified behavior which in turn will help you avoid a Catastrophic Reaction.

Today, Lou experienced the first of probably many catastrophic reactions. It was, in comparison, a relatively mild one. But one that left him and Rose further apart, and him with a weight of emotions he could not quite decipher.

In many books on Alzheimer's disease and dementia, Catastrophic Reactions are glossed over, forgotten, or disguised with the terms "aggressive" or "problem" behaviors. In reality, they are the result of caregivers, the public, family, and friends not knowing how to handle the behaviors inherent in dementia, and the confused person's inability to do otherwise.

A Catastrophic Reaction is defined as an intense response to what *seems* to be a trivial event. The dementia patient has a sudden mood change, cries, becomes verbally abusive, or even physically violent. The important piece to notice in that definition is that it's what *seems to us* to be trivial. To them, it isn't trivial at all.

Catastrophic Reactions happen when a person becomes so angry, so frustrated, or so hurt that they can only explode to relieve the overwhelming emotions. It is not a time of rational, normal behavior. And too often, these outbursts result in unnecessary institutionalization, increased home health care, hospitalizations, elder abuse, and mortality.

One of the most enduring myths of Alzheimer's and dementia is that violence is a part of its progression. It's not unusual for family members to say, "We haven't gotten to the violent stage yet." The operative word being *yet*. It's as if they assume their loved one will turn into a violent person at some point in time. This myth is perpetuated by the fact that specialized care units often have locked doors.

Anger, aggression, and frustration are all a part of each one of us. Children throw temper tantrums. Young men get into fist fights over girls. Wives nag and harp at children and husbands who don't complete their chores. We read about road rage in the papers on a daily basis. The list is endless.

All these things have one thing in common. They have a trigger event. We are reacting to something specific that happened. A child is told he can't have a certain toy. A girl flirts with another boy knowing her boyfriend won't like it. We cut each other off in traffic on a regular basis—sometimes purposefully, sometimes not.

Looking back, we can identify the exact thing that set us off, or to use an old cliché—the straw that broke the camel's back. We can identify it in ourselves and even in others we know well.

These are triggers or trigger events.

The frustrating thing about dementia patients is that their ability to analyze and rationalize what's happening to them is impaired. They cannot identify their own triggers and put them into perspective. They cannot tell us what upset them—and may not even remember getting angry.

To complicate things, we have to realize triggers are both internal and external. The driver who cut us off in traffic, the pain in our thumb when we missed the nail, the long stressful day where nothing went right—those are all external triggers.

Internal triggers are less obvious and not as easy to identify. Old memories buried in our minds are internal. There are television commercials that have managed to find a universal trigger in all of us with the sentimental commercials about home that spark tears in our eyes. We are not crying because the actors are far from an imaginary home, we are crying because a part of us misses our home and family. We identify from our own experiences.

We have all experienced past pain that may or may not come to mind when we hear or see something, but we will probably feel the emotions. These memories can be good or bad. Old anger may be stirred when someone who reminds us of a former, unfair boss walks into the room. We may not like that person because of it, and may not even realize why.

We may not ever know our own, much less each others' internal triggers. Some issues can take years of therapy to identify. The problem with internal triggers is not only in trying to identify what they are, but in controlling the external outbursts that result from them. We need to understand that triggers exist and what they are. That's the first step. The second step is to use that knowledge to try to avoid a similar catastrophic event from happening again.

While we can't always identify triggers, we can diminish their strength. If we don't, the escalation of the anger which is identified with them and their accompanying violence can increase. In a dementia patient, this result is a Catastrophic Reaction.

This doesn't have to happen. Catastrophic Reactions don't *have* to occur. They can be avoided.

When a person is angry—be they cognizant or demented—it's not a wise practice to continue pushing or arguing. We all have buttons, and react when they are pushed. That doesn't go away with the onset of dementia.

A demented person can't be reasoned with, yet people try to do it all the time.

Ask yourself if you really have to win this argument. Why? If you can't answer those questions, it's a clue to back off. If you can—ask yourself again. There is really *nothing* important enough to fight over—and that will be the result if you persist.

All beings, human and animal, have a common basic reaction to being caught in an uncomfortable or perceived dangerous situation—fight or flight.

Alzheimer's and dementia patients are no different from the rest of us. In one sense, their instincts are stronger than their minds' ability to reason the reaction away. They also have a right to the same emotions we have, yet we don't let them have that basic freedom many times.

Too often, they are pushed to the point of anger —and must decide to fight or run. They hit someone and then are called "aggressive." They run and are labeled as "exit seeking" or "wandering."

Let's explore how these catastrophic events happen.

The most useful technique during these times is the simple act of backing off. Easier said than done? Sometimes, especially when the other person is determined to get an answer or result. They may not understand why you are backing down. The element of surprise can work in your favor.

Understanding a Catastrophic Reaction is crucial to understanding all the behavior problems you'll run across in dealing with Alzheimer's and dementia patients. Any behavior, if handled inappropriately, can result in a Catastrophic Reaction. Caregivers who understand they can stay in control of a situation and deal with all behaviors are safer and better off.

Sometimes we're too close to a situation to identify it accurately, or we are too involved to objectively assess a situation. That's why tools like the *Hierarchy of Needs* from Abraham Maslow can be useful.

Maslow listed human needs in a pyramid as shown in Figure 3-1. He proposed that if the basic needs aren't met, then a person cannot progress to a higher function. If our basic needs like food, water, and physical comfort (like using the bathroom) are lacking, we focus on getting them met.

Does the dementia person need to go to the bathroom? Are they unable to find it? Are they hungry? Are they cold? Hot?

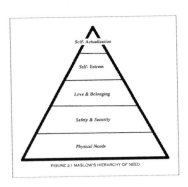

Self- Actualization

Self- Esteem

Love & Belonging

Safety & Security

Physical Needs

FIGURE 3.1 MASLOW'S HIERARCHY OF NEED

SELF-ACTUALIZATION

Look at all the basic needs. Are they met? If so, then look at the next level. Does the person feel safe?

External triggers are easiest to identify and remedy. There are also good triggers. Track those as well. They are useful in defusing a situation later.

Look around at the environment. It can be one of the most obvious and yet easily missed triggers. Have you ever sat in bumper-to-bumper traffic on a hot summer day, the car next to you blasting its radio, the air conditioner on the fritz, and your kids or the cell phone demanding your attention? It's enough to drive you over the edge.

A dementia patient has less capacity to cope. There's a reason many special care units are simple environments—some too extreme—but they've eliminated or muted a great deal of stimulation, of the possible environmental overstimulation and triggers. You can do the same by keeping televisions and radios off, or at least only have one on at a time.

You know the person you are taking care of, their likes and dislikes. None of those will change, but what will change will be their ability to voice them. For example, I detest onions. Always have, always will. My husband knows that, and often goes out of his way to inform wait staff to *not* bring me food with them in it. He's being kind to me, yes, but he's also aware he doesn't want to hear me complain, go through the whole issue of sending food back and eating a delayed meal.

If I have a caregiver someday, I hope he or she will be able to inform people of that dislike. Just because a person develops dementia doesn't mean they won't recognize an onion if they eat it.

That's the value of a history. Knowing it and sharing it with caregivers.

This brings up a controversial question. Does a demented person need to know everything about their situation? The answer is, not the overall picture about their illness, especially in the early stages, but definitely the moment-to-moment situation. Do they have to know the specific details? That, of course, will be different every time, so it's another dilemma for caregivers.

There is such a thing as Therapeutic Fibbing. People who are caregivers feel they must be one hundred percent honest with a dementia patient, something they may not have been previously. Are we all totally honest with everyone we know? Probably not. Yet why do we feel the compunction to be so with a person who has a diminished capacity, expecting them to process additional information?

If the information is something we know will upset them, or that they won't be able to do anything about anyway, then there's no reason to tell them or give specific details. This situation comes up most often when important issues arise, such as needing to tell someone about the death or illness of a loved one. But it also arises on a day-to-day basis. For instance, a favorite shirt or blouse has holes yet still, the dementia patient puts it on each morning. What spouse hasn't tossed out holey underwear or worn gardening cloths without asking? Too often, caregivers believe they need to tell the person when they are throwing out that favorite piece of clothing so they won't go looking for it.

There's nothing wrong with getting rid of the clothing, then, if asked about it, saying, "It's in the laundry. I'll wash it tomorrow." Most likely, they'll forget the clothing tomorrow. If they do remember the clothing, they won't remember your answer.

IDENTIFYING TRIGGERS

The Alzheimer's Association has a business card you can carry with you that says, "Thank you for your patience. The person with me is memory impaired and may require a few extra moments. Your understanding is appreciated." Using something like this will alleviate your need to explain, and eliminate your loved one's embarrassment as you take time to explain their "problem." If you can't find the cards, make up your own on the computer. Using this card may help eliminate unexpected triggers caused by the outside world.

Before you can detect "triggers," you must under-stand the term. Think of it like the match that lights the fire. If a volatile situation occurs, look back and see if you can identify the thing that started the whole series of events. Mark those in the journal, and brainstorm ways to avoid them happening again.

The following lists will give you ideas of how to provide an environment that is less stressful, and provide you with examples of both physical and mental triggers common to dementia patients, including a few hints for handling stressful times.

GENERAL GUIDELINES FOR CAREGIVERS

- Be upfront with friends, acquaintances, neighbors, and the public about the person's condition. It's not contagious, and nothing to be ashamed about. Other people's negative reactions may set someone off by making them feel embarrassed or judged. Dementia makes you confused . . . not stupid.
- Keep a journal of situations and events that upset the person. Is there a way to avoid those situations? A person who used to be very competent doing the checkbook may lose that ability. Don't just

say, "I'll do that from now on." Remove the reminders that they did it. Put the checkbook in another place. If possible, have statements delivered to another address.

- Try to identify what specifically upsets them. Is it the entire activity, or just a piece of it? Is it the whole bathing process or do they just dislike the cold tile? Look for patterns.

- Learn from previous experience. If they tire during big family events, limit the time and the number of people. Talk to family members beforehand and explain to them what needs to be done differently.

- Stick to a regular routine. This will cut down on the number of unexpected and stressful events they have to handle.

- If an activity or topic can be avoided, do so. If it can't be, don't do it alone. Plan for help.

- Try to make things fun for everyone, including yourself. If you look like you dread a task, they will pick up on your facial expression and body language, and will anticipate an unpleasant experience.

THE ENVIRONMENT

- Make changes gradually.
- Reduce stimulation in the environment. Avoid having more than one source of noise, e.g. music, TV, traffic noise, at a time.
- Simplify the environment. Simplify and/or decrease clutter.
- Keep heavy or sharp objects hidden, or totally remove them from the room or house.

PHYSICAL TRIGGERS

- Take note of recent medication changes. Side effects may cause mood swings. It's also possible they may not be able to tolerate certain medications.
- Watch for body language showing signs of increased discomfort. Restlessness, fidgeting, blushing, and pacing are only a few typical signs. You'll learn each person's specific signs quickly. Don't ignore them.
- Physical discomfort may cause anger. Are they in pain? Ill? Constipated or hungry? Do they need to use the bathroom? Are

they too hot or cold? Do their clothes fit
properly?
- Keep a log of sleep patterns. Fatigue may
make them more susceptible to frustration
and anger.
- Simplify tasks.
- Decrease noise.

MENTAL TRIGGERS

- Don't focus on what they can no longer do.
Learn to accept their current abilities.
Avoid reminding the person of who they
used to be if that upsets them.
- Give them limited choices, only one or
two things to choose from at a time.
- Provide verbal cues. For instance, when
you greet them, say, "Mom, it's Betty."
Don't play the guessing game of, "Do you
know who I am?" It puts the burden on
them. Take burdens, don't give them.
- *Ask* if you can help them. Allow them time
to respond. Don't automatically do
everything for them.
- Break down tasks into small steps.
- Give them adequate time to accomplish a
task or activity.
- Plan more difficult tasks for the time of
day when they are at their best.

- Offer positive reinforcement. "After your bath, we'll have a piece of pie." Follow through!
- You don't have to announce your intentions ahead of time. For instance, you can go for a walk through the house or building and stop by the bathroom. You don't have to structure everything.
- Don't talk about them as if they aren't there. Include them so they know they can ask a question or voice an opinion. Misinterpreting a conversation may upset them.
- Identify other people you bring with you. "I brought Lisa along with me today." If you told them the day before, even the hour before that you and Lisa were going to visit, don't assume they will remember. Don't ask if they remember, it simply reminds them they have a problem.
- Anger frightens them. If you're angry with someone or something, stay away, and don't try to accomplish difficult tasks until you've calmed.

HINTS FOR HANDLING STRESSFUL TIMES

- During stressful times, share an activity together that you'll both enjoy and find relaxing. Do you both like to cook? Make cookies and eat your fill. Enjoy a cup of tea? Brew a pot together and sit out on the porch in the sun.

- Avoid arguing. You won't win because they don't know they can't.
- Go for walks to burn off energy and steam.
- Plan personally meaningful activities. Offer them when their agitation increases.
- "Come with me," may work better than an explanation. Extend your hand and smile to get them to join you.
- Have the doctor write a prescription for a specific, difficult task. Keep the prescription form handy and show it to the patient when they need a reminder of the doctor's instructions.

CHAPTER 3
THE FEAR AND PARANOIA

The mall was packed. Lou hated shopping, but Rose had seen the ad in the paper and was determined to go. The thought of her on her own in the mall—especially with the recent increase in forgetfulness—made him go along.

She sat in the passenger seat with the sale ad folded neatly in her purse. They found a parking spot after three turns up and down the aisles. Lou's feet ached just thinking of the long walk ahead.

Ignoring his phantom anticipatory pains, he climbed out of the car, and followed Rose to the department store's front door. Even that short walk had him sweating. The thick black pavement gave off waves of heat, and the sun seemed to reach out and try to melt everything in sight.

Blessed coolness engulfed him as they stepped into the air conditioning.

Rose hurried ahead of him, and he quickened his steps to keep up. She nearly disappeared in the sea of bodies as she hurried toward the first rack.

He recalled all too clearly why he hated shopping.

Rose was a woman on a mission, and for the next two hours, they traipsed around and around the clothes racks in the store. She pulled outfit after outfit to show him until he felt dizzy with all the colors.

Twice, he tried to take a seat with the other hapless men who sat near the dressing room. Both times, Rose clutched his arm and pleaded with him not to leave her. Tears sparkled in her eyes, and he couldn't help glancing around at the women who threw accusing glances his way. Finally, he gave up, following along in a mindless stupor.

"That woman is too fat for that dress," Rose said suddenly and none too quietly.

"Rose!" Lou reacted to the surprising words and the woman's offended glare.

"Well, it's true."

"You can't say that."

"Say what?"

"Insult someone like that."

"Thank you," the woman who had inspired Rose's comment said across the round metal clothing rack.

"Who's she?" Rose turned on him. "Is she your girlfriend?"

"My what? Rose, how can you think such a thing?"

"Because I saw how you looked at her," Rose loudly accused him.

Lou attempted to take Rose's arm and guide her away.

She yanked her arm out of his grasp. "Don't you touch me."

"Rose, you're tired. Let's go home." Lou tried to keep his voice low.

"I'm not going anywhere with you." She began to cry, great sobs that had half the women glaring at him, the other half shaking their heads, and the two men seated near the dressing rooms looking everywhere else.

"You're cheating on me. I hate you."

"Rose, stop it." He reached for her arm again, but she stepped away and swung her purse at him. It connected with his shoulder with a solid whomp, and he stumbled.

She stared at him and Lou froze. He'd never seen a look like that in her eyes, as if she had no idea who he was, where she was, or even who *she* was.

As if she had some special radar system, she wound her way through the racks. After recovering, Lou tried to follow, but couldn't move as quickly, alternately feeling like a rat in a maze, and as if he were in one of those endless dreams where he couldn't catch up no matter how he tried.

He couldn't see her, but the gut-wrenching sobs seemed to reach over the din.

He searched and searched, unable to find her. His heart pounded in his chest. His mind reeled with all the possibilities of what could happen to her. His vision blurred, and he knew it wasn't sweat falling into his eyes. Finally, distraught and exhausted he went to the register, and had the pretty young girl there call security.

"Yes. They found a very upset woman running through the store. She is up in the office having a cool drink with the security guy."

Relief washed over Lou, and with the decrease in adrenaline, his own hurt slipped in. How could she think such a thing of him? He'd never been unfaithful, never given her reason to doubt his fidelity.

He climbed on the elevator, and slowly exited the car when the doors opened. Not only were his feelings hurt, but his shoulder ached where she'd hit him.

He found her in a tiny office with an older gentleman. He shook Lou's hand warmly. "Rose was just telling me about you. You're a lucky man to have such a proud wife."

Lou looked at Rose.

She smiled at him as if the earlier episode had never happened. He blinked. Had he imagined it? Was he going crazy?

The stiffness in his shoulder testified to the reality of their altercation.

Together, they walked to the car. Rose obviously remembered nothing.

WHEN REASONING NO LONGER WORKS

She sighed as she buckled her seat belt. "Too bad they didn't have much on sale."

Lou looked at her, then back at the road. He wasn't sure he wanted to know what had happened today.

What he did want to know was if it would happen again. That thought scared him.

IT CAN BE DISTURBING, AND FRIGHTENING TO HAVE someone you've known all your life look at you without recognition. The familiar eyes hold anger, fear, and confusion. And you have no idea what or who they are afraid of. It hurts to realize it might be you.

Consider how much more frightening it must be to sit behind those eyes. You may know you've seen this person before, or they may remind you of someone you know. Or they look like someone you believe is gone from your life, but you can't be sure.

This person is there in your personal space, doing things you generally do for yourself. They act as if they know you—and yet you don't know them . . . or maybe you do.

In the beginning, the memories may come back. Think how foolish you feel trying to remember the name of an acquaintance that slips your tongue. Mothers might run through all their kids' names and the dogs and cats, before they get the right name on a stressful day. We all feel foolish at times.

Dementia can make a person feel foolish—and frightened.

One of the first noticeable signs of dementia is a change in personality. Part of this is due to the chemical changes in the brain. Another part is due to the loss of ability to analyze the environment around them. We act the way we do by taking cues from the people and events around us.

If a person is standing in front of a large group of people, behind a podium, there is a certain type of behavior expected. Throwing food and sticking your tongue out at the people in the front row isn't on the usual list . . . unless maybe you're in fourth grade. It's not appropriate for an adult with a PhD.

With Alzheimer's, that learned behavior we acquire as we grow up is systematically erased. We can actually track it in the reverse order we learned it. Unfortunately, most of our learning is done subconsciously, and there's no written record to see what came next. What one person learns in Junior High school, another person may figure out much earlier through life experiences.

Each person is different. A very outgoing person may suddenly become shy. This may partially be due to the fact that they aren't sure what's expected of them. They can't read the cues. A normally shy person may suddenly begin cursing like a well-seasoned sailor. Those learned inhibitions are being erased.

This doesn't mean they are reliving their lives backward verbatim. It means they are following a reverse path of human development, their particular human development. It's not like running a movie backward with all the pieces intact. Memory is being erased, both good and bad. The development into adulthood is fading away; the behaviors a person will exhibit are what someone at that age would do. Not necessarily what *they* did at that age.

Traumatic events in early life may return in vivid detail. It's not unusual for grown children to learn of events from their parents' past that they never knew about. Events the parent may have even forgot about completely, or kept secret.

These, too, will eventually be erased. What may remain are the emotions those events created. The key to dealing with the person is to focus on those emotions. Keep Maslow's hierarchy in mind. For example, when they were young, during the Depression, did they go without food? Keep plenty of food around for them to see so they know it is there. Were they abused? Avoid loud voices, startling noises, or angry displays. These people especially may be fearful of closed places, such as bathrooms. Try to provide and offer something that will reassure and make them feel safe.

Another example is of a woman who had lived in Chicago during a particularly violent time in its history, in a very bad neighborhood. Someone had broken into her home when she was a child, and she lived with that fear daily. If someone else entered her room during the night, no matter how quietly, it was a guaranteed disaster. She was easily upset and could become violent because she was reliving the fear, or thought a stranger was breaking into her room. She could take hours, sometimes days, to recover.

During moments of fear and paranoia, there are several tips and techniques which can alleviate the situation for the person and for you. Try one technique. If it doesn't work, try another. Try the same technique another time. What works one day might not the next, or vice versa. Make lists of what you have tried and when. These lists will give you options, choices, and variety.

There are times which we can predict are more likely to trigger a Catastrophic Reaction. What situations might you yourself be uncomfortable in? A closed-in bathroom with someone else? An unfamiliar room or place? Someplace dark, without lighting? Try to determine what these are for the dementia patient.

WHAT TO DO

The following lists are general guidelines to be used with dementia patients. Study these so you can easily execute the skills and use them all the time. Remember, dementia patients will not understand new inventions, nor will they remember how to handle or use them.

GENERAL GUIDELINES FOR THE CAREGIVER

- Smile. A smile can calm and completely change an entire situation. It also may surprise them enough to distract them.
- Keep a sense of humor even in the most difficult situations. Humor will help you cope with the frustrations, but remember to laugh *with* them, not at them.
- Approach from the front, and in a non-threatening way. Keep your arms at your sides, not behind your back or in pockets. Position your palms forward so they can see you don't have anything to hide. Smile.
- Think ahead. Plan for situations that could upset the patient. Avoid them, if at all possible.
- Evaluate the environment. Anything can be perceived as frightening if you don't know what it is. Shadows can be very disturbing and distorting.
- If a particular situation becomes overwhelming, remove the confused person. Take them to another room or cut an outing short. If necessary, ask guests to

leave. If you've been honest with them so far, they will understand. If it's a holiday celebration, hold it at a place where there are two rooms, and family can move if necessary.

- Take time to explain to others that suspicious accusations are part of the dementing illness. Respond to the emotion or feelings behind the accusations. If it involves hurt or the death of someone who has passed away, try saying, "You really miss your mother; tell me about her."

- Look beyond the insult to the underlying message they are trying to tell you. If they ask, "Why are you trying to starve me?" it might mean "I'm hungry." "Don't lock me up," might mean "I can't find my way out of here."

- Don't get defensive if they accuse you of things you didn't do. This is normal when there are gaps in memory and confusion. Remember they aren't purposefully being malicious. They can't remember what happened or where their possessions have gone. They are protecting their self-esteem by blaming someone else.

- Maintain a calm manner when confronted with threatening behaviors. Your calm may defuse the situation and decrease their fear.

- If you, as the caregiver, become frustrated or angry, try to find someone else to handle the situation. Leave. Your anger will only increase unpleasant behavior. Just as you can read their body language, they can read yours.
- Go slow. Quick moves will make them feel unsafe and out of control. Being startled can be an almost painful experience.
- Learn or work to recall their past habits, then follow them. Did they prefer a shower or bath? Doing what they've never done before, in a way that is unfamiliar to them, makes them feel more out of control.
- Try to discover triggers for the behaviors. Make a list of them.
- Use good common sense in any situation.

- If you can't understand the verbal content of what they are saying, try to respond to the emotional content. Look at body language. What are they saying nonverbally?
- Choose short simple sentences, but speak to them as if they are adults.
- Speak slowly, and repeat if necessary. Use the same word; don't keep trying different words with the same meaning, hoping

they'll understand. It's only more
confusing for them.

- Give them time to understand, process,
  and respond to what you're asking
  of them.
- Don't bombard them with questions. Too
  many questions can increase frustration.
- Use statements rather than questions. "It's
  time to take your pills now" instead of "Do
  you want to take your pills now or after
  you eat?" *You* decide when later is.
- If the person starts to become agitated
  with a particular subject or event, gently
  change the subject or redirect the person's
  attention.

TASKS AND ACTIVITIES

The more familiar and comfortable the activity, the
greater the chance of success. Establish routines early
on in the disease and stick to them. Later, you'll find
they may be more acclimated to ways of doing things,
and more cooperative.

- Keep things simple. Complex situations
  only cause frustration and escalate
  behavior problems.

Focus on their mood and behavior rather than the
task you want or need them to complete.

- Keep reminding them of what they are doing in step-by-step terms.
- Give one instruction at a time. Break a task down into small steps.
- Think beyond the task to the environment around them. Are they modest, seldom undressing with someone around? Do they have a preferred time of day to do a specific task? Would a same-sex caregiver be preferred for intimate activities such as bathing?

FOCUSING ON THEIR MENTAL STATE

- Use positive reinforcement—food, smiles, gentle touch, personal attention, and *lots* of praise.
- Try nonverbal reassurances when possible. Holding hands, a gentle touch, or hug.
- Limit choices to two or three.
- Let the person have some sense of control. Being able to save face is important to all of us, and especially to a person who is confused.
- Keep the routine the same. Changes are upsetting since they aren't predictable, and may not be familiar. They are, therefore, particularly frightening.
- Always treat them with respect. You never

know when they will have a moment of lucidness, or what will stick in their mind. These moments can happen well into the disease.

- Don't assume they can't understand what is being said. Don't talk as if they aren't there.

- Promote a sense of security and comfort. They become frightened when they can't make sense out of the events and environment around them.

- Use familiar photos and items to remind them of current relationships. Keep them current. They won't connect you as that cute little six-year-old on the wall if you're now thirty-five.

- Label pictures with names and relationships. A caption of "Judy, daughter of Lucy" might be helpful. Don't worry about dates as time is a lost concept.

- Let them know you are there to help and protect them, to look after them. "I'm here with you. I'll take care of things."

- If they are worried about money they perceive is missing, or not having any money, let them keep change and small bills in their pockets, wallet, or a purse.

- When they are upset, distract them with an enjoyable activity. Figure out what that activity is ahead of time. Don't wait until they are upset before you go searching for that old comforter or game.

- Some people are comforted by a stuffed animal or security object, such as a sweater or blanket. Again, identify these and keep them handy.
- Try to do errands, set appointments, and run errands at non-peak hours. This may mean early morning, or at night, depending on the person. Avoid malls, especially during busy hours such as Saturday or during holiday season.
- Avoid loud or startling noises. Decrease the television volume.
- Television can scare cognitive people, and is overwhelming to dementia patients. They are often unable to separate TV from reality (consider only taped or prescreened television.)
- If they become agitated, reassure them. Face them. Make eye contact. Use gentle touch, a hug, if they will accept it. Speak softly and in a low tone. Deeper voices are easier to hear than high-pitched.

DEALING WITH VALUABLE, LOST, OR MISSING ITEMS

- Keep important documents locked up.

Make copies—several if necessary—to keep handy.

- Have precious gems replaced in valuable jewelry. Copy valuable or sentimental pictures. That way if they are lost or destroyed, you can duplicate them again and still have the original.

- Lock up valuables. Limit the amount of money a person carries. Several one-dollar bills will seem like a lot more money than a twenty.

- When items can't be found, don't scold or accuse them of hiding things. Don't try to reason with them. Instead, reassure them and help them look for their belongings. This is a good way to learn where they might think of to hide things in the future.

- Try to learn where the confused person's favorite hiding places are for storing objects which are frequently "lost."

- Carefully check clothes, baskets, hampers, and trashcans before emptying them. Make sure nothing is hidden in there that you don't want thrown away.

- Keep spares of frequently lost items like glasses, keys, hearing aids, etc. Yes, it can be expensive to have two, but much less expensive and less stressful than emergency replacements.

- Limit the number of possible hiding places

by locking drawers, cabinets, closets, or
spare rooms.

- Don't argue or insult them. Instead of
saying, "You're wrong. No one wants your
things;" say "I know you feel frightened.
I'll help you look for your things." Even if
you know you won't find what they are
looking for, look anyway. It's the action of
being on their side that will calm them and
make it easier to distract them.

BATHING

A special note about bathing, the most common time
for Catastrophic Reactions. Fear and paranoia tend
to arise during personal care—the most private
things we do. This activity can become the most
difficult time in a caregiver's week. Following are
some tips to keep in mind during this specific
activity.

- Look directly at the person. Make eye
contact so you'll know they are aware
of you.
- Speak slowly and clearly.
- Use short sentences.
- Use concrete familiar terms. Learn special
terms for objects and even body parts.
- Ask yes or no questions.
- Talk in a warm, easy-going manner

- Keep your voice at a soft tone and a low pitch.
- Don't argue.
- Listen to them.
- Stay calm and be patient.
- Begin a social conversation instead of focusing on the bath right away.
- Engage their interest in the bathing activity. Let them help prepare the bath water. Talk to them. Use their favorite bubble bath or scented bath oil.
- Pick a good time for them, as well as a familiar time. Were they a morning or evening bather throughout their life?
- Plan for a time when there is no need to rush. If the caregiver is rushed, they will pick up on that.
- If they are uncooperative, try again later.
- Consider giving them a reason for the bath. "It's Saturday night and church is tomorrow."
- Make the bathroom as inviting as possible. Is the light bright without being glaring? Is the room warm enough? Run the shower for a couple of minutes before bringing them in to warm up the air and the tile. Is the room too hot? Do you need to crack a door or window to let some of the steam out?
- Make sure you have all the things you need

to accomplish the job prepared in advance.
If you have to leave the room in the
middle, chances are they will perceive it as
finished, and you'll have to start over, or
give up.

- Consider soft soothing music to play in
  the background.
- What about bubbles? Bubble baths have
  long been associated with relaxation and
  comfort.
- Family members should not be the first
  choice to help with bathing. It's not
  normal to bathe your parent or for spouses
  to bathe each other. It's not a usual
  relationship, and is most likely a role
  change. They will be as uncomfortable
  with this as you are.
- Give them something to hold onto. A
  washcloth, a scrubby. Avoid objects, like a
  back brush, which can harmful if they
  grow upset.
- Offer to let them bathe in their underwear
  or with a towel draped over them in the
  water if they are modest.
- Consider using an assistant only as a last
  resort. If you use an assistant, make sure
  they know their role is to occupy the
  person with talk, distraction, and comfort.
  They shouldn't be there to help with the

task and make the person feel "ganged up on."

- Schedule the bath when they are already involved in a related activity, such as in the morning when they are already in the bathroom changing their clothes. Or at bedtime when they are putting on pajamas.

CHAPTER 4
CALMING THE STORM OF CONFUSION

Lou felt Rose climb from bed. The big red numbers on their bedside clock showed 1:46 a.m. He sighed, and for an instant, closed his eyes. Sleep. He needed sleep. This was the third night in a row she'd gotten up. Would it ever stop?

Rose headed to the bathroom and flipped on the light. From the bed, he could see her looking around, squinting. She didn't have her glasses on, so he knew she couldn't see well. He feared she'd trip over something and fall.

She left the bathroom and headed down the hall, flipping on lights as she went.

"Rose," he called after her, hoping the sound of his voice would break through her jumbled thoughts. She kept walking and he followed, carrying her glasses, hoping she'd take them from him.

Lights went on in every room. He turned two off.

She turned around, glared and squinted at him, then flipped the switches back on. He stopped turning them off.

She headed for the kitchen. He'd taken the precaution months ago of getting rid of all the knives and glass. But they had to eat, and he needed some tools to cook with. She headed straight for the stove.

"Melody's going to expect a cake for her birthday," she told him.

"It's not time for Melody's birthday. It's almost six months away," Lou reminded her.

"No. You don't know anything," she barked.

"Here are your glasses." He extended his hand to her. If she was going to do this, he wanted her to see clearly.

She stared at them, backing away from him. "No."

"You need them to see, Rose." He stepped closer to her, unfolding the earpieces so she could see them.

She surprised him and slapped the glasses from his hand. They hit the linoleum with a clatter. "Now look what you made me do," she yelled.

Lou moved to pick up the glasses, hoping they weren't broken. Glasses were not an expense they could afford right now. He'd barely finished paying off all the deductibles from the tests the doctor had run all those months ago.

He picked the glasses up, and slipped them into his shirt pocket then turned to face Rose. He knew he wasn't going to stop her now. He just wished she had her glasses on.

"Where's my mixer?" Rose turned around from the stove, pinning him with an angry stare. "What did you do with my mixer?"

Lou shrugged. He couldn't even remember the last time she'd used it when she was well.

"You stole it, didn't you?" She stepped toward him, pointing an accusing finger at him. "How dare you steal my things!"

"I didn't take it, Rose. It's here someplace." He knew it wasn't in any of the cupboards, but maybe if he looked, she'd remember where she'd put it.

"Don't lie to me."

"I'm not lying." Lou's strength and patience were fading. Too many nights of this took their toll. "I don't lie," he yelled back at her, angry that she'd accuse him of such a thing.

"Yes, you do."

"I don't, and you know it."

Rose backed up, her hip bumping the edge of the table where she'd set out the cake pans. She grabbed the first one and threw it at him. It hit Lou's forehead with a force that made him stumble. She grabbed the next pan as he lifted his hand to his head. He pulled his hand away and found blood on his fingers.

"Rose, don't," he commanded, finding she didn't seem to hear him. The pan hit his shoulder but not as hard as the first one.

Lou looked into Rose's face, and for the first time since she'd gotten ill, he knew that she didn't know who he was. The emptiness in her eyes scared him.

She started to scream. Words that didn't make sense, just sounds really. Sounds that seemed like fear to him.

Fear of him. He knew he was upsetting her, but he didn't know what to do. He couldn't let her destroy the kitchen.

His head throbbed, and he felt the blood trickle down the side of his face. For a minute, the room spun. He had to sit down, but if he sat on the kitchen chair, she'd hit him again.

For the first time since he'd become an adult, Lou turned and ran. He went into the guestroom and closed and locked the door.

A phone sat beside the bed. This had been Melody's room, and she'd spent hours in here talking with her friends. He grabbed the pink phone and dialed his daughter's number. After the third ring, he remembered she wasn't home. She and Jim had taken the kids to see his parents. They wouldn't be back for another week.

Panic settled into his chest, filling his lungs and making breathing nearly impossible. He sat on the bed, grabbing tissues from the box and blotting his head. The tissues soon soaked through. He blinked a couple of times to clear his sight. He dialed Julie's number. Her groggy voice answered on the second ring.

"Julie, it's Dad."

"Dad! What's the matter?"

"It's your mother. She's . . . she's upset." His voice cracked, and he tried to clear it.

"I'll be right there."

The line went dead in his hand. Lou stared at it until the obnoxious buzzing returned. Then he laid the receiver back into its cradle.

The sound of pans hitting walls and shelves echoed in his ears like cannon fire. He felt as if he were living in a battlefield. The land mines kept blowing up around him. For the first time, he thought he might not win.

Every light in the house burned. Julie heard the noise halfway up the sidewalk. She walked around the side of the house and stood there in the darkness, staring. Her mother was in the middle of the usually immaculate kitchen, throwing everything she could get her hands on into the sink. It overflowed, so that every new item she put on top fell to the floor with a clatter.

The water was turned on full blast and dripped over the edge of the sink. It crackled loudly when it hit the linoleum.

Where was Dad? He'd sounded so awful. She continued on, heading around to the back door. It was locked. She knocked, but either no one heard her over the racket, or her mother chose to ignore her. Where was Dad? The question repeated itself in her head as she dug through her purse for her key.

Julie pushed the door open, the familiar creak of

the hinges nearly drowned out by the water and falling pans. Her mother looked up and smiled.

"Hello, dear. How was your day?"

Julie could only stare as Rose grabbed a dishcloth and proceeded to wash the mountain of dishes. She seemed totally oblivious to anything else. She even hummed.

"Where's Dad?" Julie took a tentative step into the room.

"Oh, he should be home from work soon. Why don't you get started on your homework?" Rose kept scrubbing the dishes.

"Homework?" Julie whispered. Her mother seemed content for the moment to wash dishes, and Julie let her. She stepped into the hall and called for her father. He didn't answer. Panicked, she began a room-by-room search. When he wasn't in the master bedroom or the bathroom, tears filled her eyes. Had something happened to him? Where was he?

A sound coming from Melody's room startled her. She moved toward it, ready to run if need be. The door opened slowly, and her father's big, tall figure filled the cracked opening. She rushed to him, thankful he was okay.

But he wasn't okay. Blood stained his face and his shirt. He had a pillowcase wadded up in his hand and pressed to his forehead. She felt the warmth drain from her own face.

"Daddy?" She hurried toward him, not knowing

what to do. Her mother seemed content to keep washing dishes, oblivious to her father's pain.

Lou opened the door and let her in. She noticed he closed the door behind him—and locked it.

"What happened?"

"Your mom was upset. She threw a pan at me." He sat down on the bed beside Julie, and for the first time in her entire life, she was at a loss. He'd never been the one who needed help before. Never needed anyone for that matter, except Mom.

She took a deep breath. "Let me look at that." She pulled the fabric away, relieved to find that most of the bleeding had stopped. "Let me clean that up."

"No." He grabbed her hand. "She's upset."

"Not anymore," Julie reassured him. Leaving the bedroom, she slipped into the bathroom down the hall and grabbed the first aid kit, then slipped back into the bedroom without her mother noticing a thing. Lou insisted she lock the door.

After they'd cleaned the wound and his face, Lou slipped off his shirt. The thin T-shirt underneath would do until he could get back to his room and change.

Julie noticed the droop in his shoulders and the fatigue in his face. She looked away from his eyes, not strong enough to face his pain.

"It's quiet out there." She stepped to the door. She turned the lock and slowly pulled the door open. Lou stood right behind her, and she could feel his uncertainty along the back of her neck as they returned to the kitchen. She felt like the mother quieting her son's fears about the boogieman.

Sound asleep in the middle of the mess, Rose sat hunched at the table, her arms crossed beneath her chin. The water still ran in the sink. Pots and pans lay scattered across the floor and counters.

Julie watched her father hesitate, then turn back around, the fear gone from his eyes. Instead, tears filled his eyes, and he slumped against the counter . She didn't know what to do.

She walked to the sink and turned off the water, then she heard the first sob break from her father's chest. The door closed softly, and she knew he didn't want her to see him like this. She also knew she couldn't leave.

Carefully and quietly, she picked up the pots and pans and started putting them away. Rose's quiet breathing was the only sound beside her footsteps. When she'd finished drying the counters and the floor, Julie sat down at the table across from her mother's sleeping figure.

"Oh, Mama." Her tears finally came, and the first one had just fallen onto her cheek when a warm strong hand closed over her shoulder. Lou pulled her into his arms. "We have to do something don't we?" she whispered against his chest.

Lou nodded, knowing it was time for another visit to the doctor. Rose wasn't going to like it, but he was beyond the point of being able to do what Rose liked anymore.

Now you know what Catastrophic Reactions are and how to identify the triggers. But, how do you deal with them? There's no perfect solution, and while you can diminish the Catastrophic Reactions, you can't completely avoid them.

There's nothing more frightening than looking into eyes you've looked into for years and seeing nothing. No recognition. No smile. Nothing—except maybe fear.

They try. You can see them struggling to figure out who you are. Where they are. The frown deepens on their brow. They pace. They wring their hands. When the answer continues to elude them, they grow frustrated and angry.

You ask yourself, will they cry, will they get angry, will they walk away? Will their face suddenly clear, to give you a dazzling smile? There's no way of knowing for sure, especially in the beginning.

But you can learn to predict their reactions and even circumvent them much of the time.

There *are* ways to guide them, to avoid the full-blown Catastrophic Reaction. But what happens when this is the first time you've faced this situation? Or maybe it's not the first, but you still don't know what to do. This chapter will give you ideas of what to do and how to do it. Ways you can try to protect your loved one, your family and yourself from heartache and pain—both emotional and physical.

Lou reacted the same way most of us would. He tried to make Rose fit into the real world, a world where it's the middle of the night, it's six months away from the day she thought it was (or maybe six months and several years away) and it's a place where she recognizes and trusts him.

For Rose, that world no longer exists.

In the past, a practice called Reality Orientation was used. This is a technique where the caregiver keeps reminding the patient of where they are, what time it is, etc. This is usually a waste of time, and very frustrating for both the patient and caregiver. Is it really necessary that the person know what day and time it is?

Naomi Feil, a social worker who specializes in working with the confused elderly, wrote a book in 1982 that described a program called Validation Therapy. Validation Therapy is based on simple principles and is a more successful and humane way of dealing with behaviors.

In Feil's book, she says, "To validate is to acknowledge the feelings of a person. To validate is to say that their feelings are true. Denying feelings invalidates the individual. Validation uses empathy to tune into the inner reality of the disoriented. Empathy, or walking in the shoes of the other, builds trust. Trust brings safety. Safety brings strength. Strength renews feelings of worth. Worth reduces stress. With empathy, the Validation Worker picks up their clues and helps put their feelings into words. This validates them and restores dignity." (See Appendix C.)

This humanistic type of therapy and its premise have been widely used in long-term care facilities for years. I'm not suggesting that a home caregiver learn and use a full therapy program, but many of the practices and techniques can be incorporated into your daily interactions. They've been used to avoid Catastrophic Reactions with consistent success.

Let us look at the situation between Rose and Lou. We are all aware how tired Lou is during all this. Odds are Rose is tired, too, on some level. But something is making her restless and keeping her awake.

Lou feels it's important that she wear her glasses, but his first interaction with her was very telling—he turned off lights, and she glared at him. That was the first clue she was upset. He might have said something like, "Oh, you want the lights on. I didn't know. I'm sorry I turned them off." This would reassure her that what she was doing was okay.

As she went about the kitchen to bake the cake, rather than pointing out that the birthday isn't here yet, he could have asked what kind of cake she's going to make, keeping his tone light and matter-of-fact.

Forget it's the middle of the night or let yourself yawn, yawn on purpose. Send signals that it's a time to be tired.

When Rose continues to be determined to make the cake, Lou can offer to help. He could ask, "Would you like your glasses?" She may realize she needs them and take them. It's a small thing, but it allows her to have control.

If this is your situation and she lets you help make the cake—make the cake. If you're like Lou and Rose and don't have everything, look for it. Offer to go through the cupboards. If you are accused of stealing, don't get angry and defensive. You can ignore the accusation, and say, in a matter-of-fact manner, that you'll help find the item because you know how important it is to her.

Remember that an argument with anyone with dementia is simply that. There is no win or lose because in time, they won't remember. Is it so important that you "win" and that they know you are right and they are wrong?

As Rose's behavior continues to escalate, she isn't getting sleepy, she hasn't accepted the glasses, and she has continued to get angry about the mixer. It's time to change tactics.

Remain calm. Try to make eye contact. Ask simple questions about something pleasant. Lou might have asked Rose about the daughters' birthdays. Something special. "Melody sure does love ripping open her presents, doesn't she?" Direct the conversation to beautiful and pleasant things.

As you talk, stay with simple yes or no questions. Don't ask for deep complex thoughts, especially when they are upset. This will only overwhelm them and add to their frustration.

Validate their feelings. Former roles in life

provided proof of worth. Dementia often steals those roles, and along with them, self-worth. Give some of that back by reminding them of it. "Melody sure loves your cakes. You're such a good mom to her and the other kids." Acknowledge her and her feelings as valid and important.

"I'm right here, Rose. I'll help you," would have possibly defused her anger. "I'll be here with you all night" goes further.

Just his body language would speak to her. Since he was angry, his stance was probably rigid and threatening. A softer voice, relaxed stance, with an offered friendly hand would do so much more.

Use validation and watch to see if their needs are being met. You will find your observations helpful, even in the middle of a crisis.

There will be times when no matter what you do or say, you can't calm them. We all make mistakes. We aren't perfect. Even knowing the techniques, we may be too tired or overworked and miss cues. That's okay. Recovery is possible.

Lou did the only thing possible—he backed off. It's important to remember that keeping you and them safe must be the main goal. If something happens to you, there's no one else to take care of them.

Only one person should deal with an upset dementia patient. If more people are around, make sure they back off and stay away. More than one person and the dementia patient may feel ganged up on. Two against one is never fair, even when we were kids. The only choice then is to run or fight, neither of which you want them to choose at this point.

The last thing to worry about is property. If all they are going to do is mess up a room, let them. "Stuff" can be replaced, and dangerous items should have already been removed from the environment. A room can be cleaned up later. Yes, it's more work, but healing a damaged body is worse.

Sometimes, just leaving them alone for awhile without you, without any added stimulation, will do the trick. Sometimes we just need our solitude, especially when we're uncomfortable. They will probably calm themselves, using up their energy, and do as Rose did, sitting down to sleep.

You can often go into the next room where you can keep an eye on them, yet they don't realize you're there. Quiet and solitude are great stress reducers, and Catastrophic Reactions are illustrations of major stress.

Staying calm is the most important and most difficult thing to do during a Catastrophic Reaction. If you find you can't do it, if the situation is beyond your abilities, call for help. Call a neighbor, a friend, family, or, if needed, 9-1-1.

Yes, there will be consequences, but at least you'll be healthy enough to deal with those consequences. Too many times a caregiver has gotten sick or hurt and can't deal with the decisions ahead. Don't lose control of your life by losing control of the moment. A disaster may be only one mistake away.

HOW TO USE VALIDATION

PHYSICAL VALIDATIONS

- Watch body language, yours for sending out the wrong signals, and theirs for clues to how they feel.
- Approach them in a calm, non-threatening manner. Hands at sides, palms out. Don't put your hands behind your back or in your pockets. It looks as if you're trying to hide something.
- Smile often to reassure the person you aren't angry and to remind you to stay calm. Speak in a normal, calm tone of voice.
- Allow the person to verbalize their feelings.
- Alleviate their fears. "I'll take care of that for you." "Melody knows you're here with me."
- Use a matter-of-fact, casual approach.

- Use gestures, done slowly and carefully, as part of your communication.
- Remain calm.
- Provide a quiet atmosphere.
- When the patient is agitated, leave them alone for five to ten minutes, if safe. Watch from a distance, if necessary, to ensure safety.
- Allow the person to sit with you in a calm, loving way. Give them a hug; hold hands.
- Keep pretty, favorite pictures handy. Ask them who or what's in the picture.
- Offer to help them, even if the task seems incongruous to you.
- Allow the person to verbalize their feelings. Ask related but distracting questions. For example, if they are doing as Rose was, wanting to bake a cake for her daughter's birthday, Lou could have asked her, "What kind of cake are you going to make?" Follow that with "Melody liked your cakes. You're such a good mother to her."
- Provide empathic acceptance of feelings. "It must be difficult."
- Compliment them for completion and attempts at tasks.
- Reassure them that they are safe.
- Reassure the person that you will stay with them.

- Avoid people or things the person doesn't like.
- Give them something comforting to hold. A teddy bear, cookie, pillow.

VERBAL VALIDATIONS

- Ask simple yes or no questions.
- Avoid asking complicated questions that require an abstract answer.
- Discuss pleasant thoughts.
- Reminisce; discuss their past life.
- Ask them to describe a pleasant, relaxing memory. If they can't come up with one, suggest one that they are likely to be pleased by. Ask them to embellish. Childhood is a fertile ground for such memories. Remind them of being a kid on the front porch eating a Popsicle. What does the person love? The beach? Talk about the sand and the sound of the surf and warm sunshine.
- When they call out for someone not there, or even someone who's dead, don't remind them that the person is gone. Talk about that person in a nice way, and do something that person would do, e.g., pat an arm, give a hug. Redirect conversation to a positive topic.

- Help them look for things they believe are missing.
- Ask them to repeat your instructions back to you. Don't force it or scold them if they get it wrong. Gently repeat the instructions and allow them time to process the information.

PREVENTING A CATASTROPHIC REACTION

- Remove environmental stressors and triggers. Keeping track will help you identify what these are.
- Remove unsafe objects (even canes and walkers if you feel they will be used harmfully.)
- Give beautiful moments, smile, laugh, and provide beauty.
- Use TLC and affection generously.
- Show interest in what they are trying to do or say.
- Show them deep-breathing exercises. Do them. They may mimic your actions. It will calm you both.
- Consider aromatherapy. Different scents are very comforting and soothing, to both

of you. It encourages sleep and positive, relaxed mood shifts.

- Use a nightlight that has an aromatherapy pad. Lavender oil is very relaxing. The light helps them relax and the oil soothes.
- Put cotton balls soaked in lavender oil in your pocket. It's relaxing for everyone.
- Massage feels good to anyone; just be sure they accept touch and be gentle.
- Keep favorite activities available at all times.
- Avoid trying to teach. Offer encouragement, but keep in mind their abilities, and don't expect more than they can do.
- Provide safe, yet meaningful tasks. Feather dusters, folding clothes, unscrewing nuts and bolts (and then reconnecting them). If you use a mop or broom, be careful, as they can become weapons. Washing dishes can be very calming and time filling.
- Avoid having them continually perform a particular task if they repeatedly are unsuccessful. If it's difficult for them to button a shirt, remove the shirt and hand them a pair of pants. Go back to the shirt later. Consider changing their wardrobe to eliminate buttons, or other difficult fasteners.
- Provide a safe way to release frustration. A

punching bag perhaps? You can also use one of those blow-up children's toys that bounces back when it's punched.

- Buy balloons to bat around. That will burn off frustration and energy. It's fun for both of you.

- Is the person hungry? Offer favorite, comfort and/or finger foods—warm milk and cookies,. decaffeinated coffee and tea, peanut butter sandwiches.

- Does the person need to go to the bathroom? Direct them there. Mark these rooms with signs and/or pictures to help them find them on their own. Painting the door a contrasting color to the rest of the wall is also helpful.

- Are they too hot? Too cold? Offer a sweater or turn on cool air. Avoid offering coats or similar clothing that will indicate they may be going someplace. Open or close windows if the person is too hot or too cold. Remember to only open them far enough to let a breeze in, not provide an escape route.

- Time medications to avoid times of day where they are more exhausted or resistant.

- Stick with bedtime routines as much as possible Rocking chairs are solid and may help to relax them.

- If there is a chiming clock in the house, stop the chimes if possible, especially if there is a particular time that upsets them. Some people, who have worked a swing shift all their lives, become agitated when the clock strikes three o'clock. Remind them it's their day off. You don't have to tell them they are retired. Loss of important roles can be upsetting.
- Colors can increase or decrease moods and reactions. Avoid wearing red or other hot colors like orange that can increase anger and mood. Green is calming, as is the person's favorite color.
- Does the house have dimmer switches? Turning them down can calm, and at night, it signals the end of the day.
- Animals provide unconditional love that doesn't require verbal communication. Encourage interaction with animals through a pet or a friend's pet.
- Go for a walk with them, inside or outside. Walking and moving around uses up energy and calms them.
- Go for a ride in the car. "We don't have any eggs." Look in the fridge. "Let's go to the store and get some." Maybe the process of getting shoes, coat, etc. will change their train of thought.
- Try written reassurances for a mildly

impaired person, such as "Melody will be here at 2:00 to pick you up." Keep them in a familiar notebook or use a dry erase board in a spot they pass frequently.

BEHAVIORS TO AVOID

- Don't try to orient the person to the here and now. They can't understand it, and will only grow frustrated. Reality Orientation can too easily become reality confrontation.
- Don't point out the negative behavior to the person or reprimand them for doing or saying the wrong thing.
- Don't discount or try to talk the person out of their feelings, even if their feelings seem inappropriate to the situation.
- Don't try to lessen the loss of people, things, life roles, or abilities.
- Don't provide false hope. Either say nothing, or change the subject.
- Don't argue with them, even if what they are saying or doing is incorrect.
- Don't scold or correct actions or behaviors.
- Don't yell or speak loudly.

- Don't get close to them unless you are sure they can accept it.
- Avoid getting in front of their feet or legs where it's easy for them to kick you either accidentally or on purpose. If you are helping them put on shoes, do it from the side, not directly in front of them.
- Avoid taking their aggression personally. Remember that it's the disease.
- Avoid late-night TV. It can be quite violent and disturbing. Avoid any TV that can be emotional. Soap operas, the news, and dramas, especially. Videotapes are more easily controlled.
- Avoid all clocks if at all possible. Wear a sturdy watch if you must know time. Often time references make them think they are late for something.
- Avoid breezes and wind, natural or man-made. For some reason, they increase agitation. Even those of us who are cognitively fine can find them irritating.
- Avoid mirrors. They often don't recognize themselves and will become frightened; also, they reflect light and give a false sense of space, which can make them uncomfortable.
- Avoid shiny surfaces like slick waxed floors, especially in places where sunshine will glare in the morning or late afternoon.

Bright light is painful and can startle them enough to cause a fall.

- Don't offer food at bedtime that's normally a part of the morning wake-up routine, e.g., a bowl of cereal or toast.
- Caregivers should avoid wearing long necklaces or earrings. Men shouldn't wear ties. They can be grabbed and used to hurt you, on purpose and accidentally.

WHAT TO DO DURING A CATASTROPHIC REACTION

During a catastrophic event in which they are not calming down, keep in mind the basic hierarchy. If all they are going to do is harm furniture, is it that important or can it be replaced? Most *things* can be. Heirlooms should be removed ahead of time, or stored somewhere safe. Step back and let them calm on their own. If they are going to hurt another person, remove the other person. Don't try to remove the upset person. If they are going to hurt you, *leave.* You aren't any good to anyone if you get hurt.

HANDLING A CATASTROPHIC REACTION BEFORE IT ESCALATES

- Gather, list, and identify comforting items which carry positive memories. Many of us had a blanket or special toy as a child that comforted us. That comfort continues. Stuffed animals, dolls, and blankets are still comforting, even to adults.
- Limit the number of people around the person. If one person can handle it, all others need to leave the room but stay nearby in case they are needed.
- Remove other people and animals from the room until they calm down.
- Introduce a new person to the situation, then step back.
- Make eye contact and make sure they focus and see you before touching them.
- It may help to say, "Please stop."
- Ask them to help you with something somewhere else.
- Acknowledge their feelings. "I know you're tired and frustrated."
- Try favorite, calming music played softly in the background.
- Comfort foods might also distract. Ice cream? A cup of tea? Going out for coffee, away from the upsetting situation (decaf is

best.) A grilled cheese sandwich and tomato soup have been voted one of the most popular comfort food meals. Much of the value in chicken soup is the comfort.

- Don't be embarrassed by their behavior. You are not responsible or in control of them. Neither are they.
- Stay calm. Be patient and understanding. Provide reassurance but don't argue.
- Repeat reassurances. Short-term memory is damaged and won't pass information into long-term memory, especially if they are stressed and upset.
- Back off and try later. Stay flexible. There are few things that need to be done immediately. You are capable of adapting or changing to situations more than the person in your care is.

WHAT TO DO IF THEY BECOME COMBATIVE

When a Catastrophic Reaction happens, you have two choices—remove the person from the room, or leave the room and give them time to calm down. If you must leave them, be sure the environment is safe before you do so. Don't go far. Monitor them for a time, then return as if nothing had happened. Avoid reminders of their earlier behavior. If the person is receptive to leaving, take or guide them to a quiet room away from the area where they are upset. Have a cup of tea. Go for a walk. Distract them.

In either situation, the following list of guidelines should be used to calm the person and neutralize the situation.

- Always keep in mind that *you* must remain in control of yourself, if not the situation. They need you.
- Speak slowly and clearly. If you must repeat what you say, use the same words and tone.
- Approach slowly and from the front.
- Make eye contact on the person's level. If they are seated, lower yourself to their level.
- Stay out of their personal space. If they are upset, double or even triple the size of that space. Arm's length at least.
- Give one-step instructions. Break requests and activities into manageable tasks.
- Try to use touch to reassure and comfort the person. TLC goes a long way.
- Hold out your hand as if you are shaking their hand or ask them to take your hand.
- Offer another, safer task. "I'll get the cake stuff ready while you fold these towels."
- Experiment with objects that are soothing, such as stuffed animals.
- Suggest a warm bath if they are receptive.

- Sing a song. Sing several songs.
- Begin singing their favorite song. Hum it if you don't remember the words. Don't worry about the quality of your voice; it's the familiarity that will soothe them.
- Use repetition and frequent reminders.
- Yawn—it's contagious.
- If they are throwing things, hand them pillows or foam toys. Learn to duck and try to move ahead of them and remove things that can be harmful to them or you.
- Remember, they aren't necessarily angry with you. They may have misunderstood a situation, or they may be frustrated by their own limitations.
- Avoid showing anger or impatience in your voice or body language. Use please, thank you and "Don't worry, everything will be fine."
- Try to ignore the angry behavior if distraction and support don't work.
- Let them scream. If you really can't handle it, offer them food like finger foods, hard candy, or ice cream.
- Ignore foul language. It's not personal.
- If they grab your hair, push down on their knuckles to break their hold.
- Be conservative in using restraint or force unless the situation is serious or dangerous. Avoid holding or physically

restraining them. Fighting with them will only increase their—and your —frustration.

These are but a few suggestions. With each situation, with each person, new options can be discovered and used. Be aware that what works once, might not work again. Some actions might always succeed, others have to be revised or changed.

After a situation has concluded, and you have a minute to take a breath and think, recount all the events, write everything down. What started the situation; what made them more agitated; what calmed them. Learn to identify what set them off (the trigger) so you can avoid it happening again. Learn from your trip-ups and fumbles. They aren't mistakes if you learn something from them.

Awareness of the situation, and awareness of your options, are your most valuable tools.

CHAPTER 5
LOST IN FAMILIARITY

Rose turned off the vacuum, and the sudden silence seemed heavy. The house was empty, of course. It was the middle of the day. Lou was at work and the kids, well, they were at school or work or something. She frowned a minute. She wasn't totally sure. She'd have to ask Lou when he came home.

A loud thud startled her, and she dropped the vacuum's cord. The noise had come from outside and she rushed to the window. The bright sunshiny day lifted her spirits, but when she looked across the street she froze.

A young man, his long brown hair loose about his shoulders, carried a television out of her neighbor's front door. The thud she'd heard had been the screen slamming closed. He hefted the large TV into the bed of a battered pickup truck. He turned and headed back to the front door.

"Oh dear," Rose whispered. She hugged herself. What should she do? First, she rushed to the front door and twisted the deadbolt. Slowly, carefully, she checked all the windows, making sure they were closed and the locks solid. Next, she headed to the back door and made sure the bolt was solid there, then slid the chain across as well.

She locked the door to the garage. It wasn't as strong a lock, and she slid the heavy waste can in front of it. At least, if someone tried to come in, she'd hear them.

Comforted by her actions, she went back into the living room. She looked out the window, then realized he might see her and quickly drew the drapes. She peeked through a narrow opening and watched.

The man carried out several boxes and stacked them beside the truck. Then he and another young man carried out a bed frame. Were they going to take everything her neighbor owned? Why didn't someone call the police?

Should she call the police? Panicked, she raced around looking for the phone. Where was it? It wasn't on the desk in Lou's den like it had always been when she was a girl. She stopped in the hall. No, that wasn't right? Was it?

Her heart raced and she decided the best thing to do was to keep an eye on the man. If he came to rob her house, she'd do something then. Yes. That sounded like a plan.

She parted the drapes just an inch and pulled the

desk chair up to the opening. Holding a pillow from the couch tight, needing something to comfort her, she sat and watched. Over the course of the afternoon, the man filled the truck and drove away, coming back twice for another load.

5:30 p.m. Time to *finally* go home. Lou let the tension of the day slip away as he climbed into his truck and started the engine. He had called Rose at lunch time and she said she had been vacuuming. She'd seemed more with it this morning and he'd felt good all day. He looked forward to spending some time with her this evening.

He flipped on the air conditioning as he sat in traffic, anticipating the cool comfort of the house and a tall glass of iced tea.

He pulled into the drive, punching the garage door opener. Nothing happened. What the . . . ? Great. He'd have to call the company to check it. Maybe it was something simple like a pulled plug. He parked in the drive and headed around to the front door.

The kid across the street was loading the last of his things in the truck. Lou remembered he'd planned to move to his own apartment this week. He'd been over the evening before, regaling Lou and Rose with the details of his big move. He'd been so excited, and Rose had enjoyed their conversation.

Lou waved at John and pushed on the front door. Nothing happened. Locked? Rose never locked the door during the day if she was home. Panic shot through him. Had she gone somewhere? He knocked with one hand as he held the screen open with his shoulder, and fished for his keys in his pocket.

She didn't answer his knock, so he unlocked the door. "Rose?" The urgency in his voice made it seem extra loud in the small room.

"Oh, Lou." She came running out of the bedroom. Tears streamed down her face. She flung herself at him. He dropped his lunchbox, his keys, everything in a clatter to the wood floor.

"Hey, what's the matter?"

"There's a thief in the neighborhood." She pulled away, hastily shoved the door closed behind him, and locked it. She nearly stumbled over his keys but didn't seem to notice.

"Rose what happened? What are you talking about?"

"He's been here all afternoon. I didn't know what to do. I don't think the people across the street have a single thing left."

Lou relaxed. John. "Oh, sweetheart, that's not a thief. That's John. Their son. He's moving out to his own apartment."

"No. Lou, you're wrong. That boy who lives across the street is barely starting school." Her voice was shrill, and Lou noticed her lips were thinned. "I'm here all day long. You're at work. You don't know what goes on around here."

"I know what's going on, Rose. John came over here just a couple of nights ago." Lou bent to pick up his things so neither of them tripped. "He told us all about the new apartment, remember?"

She was silent for a minute then shook her head. "No, Lou. You don't understand." She glared at him as if he'd lost his mind. "No. They'll come in and get us."

"Don't be ridiculous, Rose." It was hotter than heck in here. She'd obviously had the windows closed up all day and no air conditioning on. He reached for the curtains and pulled them open. Rose shrieked.

Frowning, Lou backed up. He could only stare. She rushed back across the room, yanking the curtains closed again. He heard a soft rip and looked up to see the fabric torn at the top. "What are you doing? You tore the curtains."

"It's too much," she screamed, as if that explained everything.

"Too much what?"

"Stop it!"

He stepped away from her, a shiver shooting up his spine. He left the window and headed to the thermostat. He turned on the air conditioning and she didn't even seem to notice. It might take a while, but the house would cool off soon. If not, it would when the sun went down, and they could go outside and sit on the front porch.

He watched Rose turn away from the window and sit down on the couch. She huddled there, but when he moved toward her, she looked up at him, her eyes filled with fear and pain.

Suddenly, she hopped up from the couch, and

hurried into the kitchen as if she'd remembered something she forgot to do. Lou followed behind.

In the middle of the kitchen, Rose leaned against the heavy oak table, trying with little success to move it. Two chairs on the opposite side fell to the tile floor.

Lou took a deep breath to ease his racing heart and breathing. "What are you doing?"

She looked at him and jumped away from the table. "He's been here. He'll come back."

Her tears started anew, and the ache in Lou's chest nearly crippled him. He stepped toward her and she stepped back.

"Everything's fine." He tried to soothe her, and while she didn't move away from him, she didn't move closer. "It's okay, hon. I'm here now. No one's going to hurt you."

Before he could take another step, she opened her mouth and let out a blood-curdling scream. Lou nearly screamed himself in frightened response. He had no clue what to do, but realized he wasn't making things better by getting any closer.

Lou turned away not knowing what else to do except leave her alone. He headed to the bedroom and his afternoon shower.

As the water sprayed down over his exhausted and overheated body, he closed his eyes and swallowed the tightness in his throat. One of the things he'd always loved about Rose was her fearlessness, her willingness to trust people. The emptiness and fear in her eyes, the lost look, tore at his heart. While it had only been for a moment, was it a taste of what was to come?

Dressed and feeling fresh and relaxed for the first time all day, Lou returned to the kitchen. It looked just as he'd left it. Or so he thought at first. Then he realized the back door stood wide open.

Fear settled deep inside him. "Rose?" There was no answer, just the soft sigh of the wind as it came in the door and chilled him clear to the bone.

He ran to the back door and nearly collapsed in relief. She was walking out in the garden. Pacing, back and forth. The stiffness of her stance told him she was still upset. So, he stood there, watching and waiting while his heart returned to its earlier, calmer pace.

PROBABLY THE HALLMARK BEHAVIOR OF DEMENTIA, and more specifically Alzheimer's disease, is wandering. That behavior where the person seems to be in constant motion, going to some unidentifiable place. They can't be reasoned with. They sometimes don't even seem to realize you're there. They are often unstoppable.

It is the one behavior which can force institutionalization. Locked and secured units were designed for Alzheimer's victims and were created specifically to deal with this behavior.

No medication can stop wandering, and few interventions will alleviate it. It is a stage of the disease which is only resolved when the next stage of decline arrives and the body is physically unable to move anymore. Even then, there are times the body and brain don't get the message, and the person continues to try to get up and wander.

Injuries are common and should be expected.

In an earlier scene with Rose and Lou, Rose left him in a public place, getting separated in a strange place which can happen to anyone at different times.

Wandering doesn't happen only in strange places. It is a behavior that can occur in familiar places such as the home. It can be aimless wandering within the house, or wandering away from it in search of something or someone. Sometimes, it is even in the search of "home." In these cases, home isn't a place but a feeling they are looking for.

Just as with other behaviors we've discussed previously, wandering has triggers which can be identified. Patterns can be documented, and a plan created to help alleviate the need to wander.

A term coined by those working in Alzheimer's care is Sundowning. This is a term used to describe the phenomenon of increased behaviors and emotional upheavals that occur as the day fades into evening. Wandering is often one of the behaviors most strongly affected by Sundowning.

Oftentimes, wandering increases or begins at this

time of day. Other behaviors, such as combativeness, also increase at this time.

Many factors may contribute to Sundowning. Late afternoon is where the day winds down. Fatigue affects many of us, and increases our irritability.

Traditionally, it is also a time when our day is over; we head home from work, shift gears, and move at a different pace. It may be difficult for a dementia victim, who still thinks they should be shifting gears later in the day as well. The pace doesn't seem to change as it should. They may wonder when they get to end their day. The cognitive decline makes then unable to realize they are now retired, their children are gone, and they no longer have the responsibilities they left behind.

It's important for caregivers to understand that wandering is a behavior to expect and to prepare for. It may or may not occur. Not all dementia or Alzheimer's victims wander. Many, however, do.

This behavior, just like all other behaviors, is not meant personally, and caregivers need to remind themselves not to take it that way. They aren't trying to necessarily get away from you. They may be trying to get away from what you are trying to make them do, but it's not you. More likely they are trying to find, or get *to,* someone or something they believe is waiting for them. A family member. A friend. An appointment. A task they believe was left undone.

Or they are searching for a solution to a problem they can't quite understand. Like where the bathroom is, or finding food to eat that they recognize. Modern technology is wonderful, but if a person believes they are in the 1940s and sees a modern invention, they might not even recognize its purpose. Everything from toilets to yogurt containers looks drastically different from what it did fifty years ago. They may need to be told what common ordinary things are for.

Wandering bothers caregivers more than it does the wanderer. The wanderer takes it in stride, and believes they are supposed to be doing what they are doing. The only time it becomes a problem is when someone tries to stop them.

So the first question is, do they need to be stopped?

Is it bothering or endangering them? Then yes, intervene. Or, if you can help them solve the problem that is initiating it, then yes, intervene. New environments can also trigger wandering. Nothing is familiar, so they will go looking for it.

But if they aren't in danger and seem content to move around, let them. Another reason they may be wandering is simply the restlessness we all feel when we've been inactive too long. When the day outside is too sunny to be inside, or too dark and cool, it makes anyone experience cabin fever. Sometimes it just feels good to get up and stretch your legs.

Try to differentiate why they are walking around. Then discern if it's actually something you need to worry about. Just because they are up walking around doesn't necessarily make it a bad thing.

Follow them or even join them on an enjoyable walk. You might be surprised how much you need the break and exercise.

Once wandering begins, it's too late to be prepared. Prepare ahead of time. There are two important steps to take. First, register anyone diagnosed with dementia with Safe Alert through the Alzheimer's Association. The toll free 800 number has saved many lives and many stressful hours (see Appendix D).

At one facility I worked in, a couple of women brought a gentleman in who had been walking up a very busy four-lane street. They thought perhaps he was from our facility. He wasn't. He didn't have any identification, but he could tell me his name. I took a chance and called the 800 number. That name was in their registry. Within minutes, the operator had patched me into his home and I was giving directions to a very distraught wife.

Her sons were out in cars and on foot searching, their minds spinning with worry, panic and guilt.

Within fifteen minutes, she and her sons arrived. The gentleman couldn't understand what all the fuss was about, but his wife knew. His sons knew.

Without that 800 number, we might not have been able to reunite that family. Call and register them today. There's information on how and where to get registration information in Appendix D.

The second step is to put together an emergency kit. Keep a current close-up picture of the dementia victim in it; a video tape would also be a good idea. Keep a list of their hair color, eye color, height, and weight. Keep a current list of emergency numbers, including neighbors, local businesses and friends, family, and organizations—anyone who might be able to help search or who they would go to.

You'll never know when they will wander away. You can't predict it, so there's no need to blame yourself when it happens. Some people wander and come back. Others can't find their way from the bathroom to the bedroom. Some do it incessantly, not even stopping for sleep. When they wander, be prepared to search for them. There are several tips below which can help before, during, and after such an episode.

WHAT TO DO TO PREVENT OR DIMINISH WANDERING: GENERAL GUIDELINES

- Visit the doctor if wandering starts suddenly. There's no medication to stop wandering, but underlying medical conditions may make them uncomfortable or restless.
- Let the police know you have an

Alzheimer's person in your home and that they may wander. If possible, the usual police officers in your neighborhood might be able to meet the person ahead of time.

- Inform the neighbors that they may wander. Keep their names and phone numbers handy. You may have to educate them on the disease, and what techniques to use on how to approach the person.
- Keep a recent, good clear photo, or make a video.
- Set routines early in the illness. Go to day care when they can understand it and adjust to it as normal. Start with small time frames and expand. Keep to routines as much as possible.

IDENTIFICATION WITH PERSONAL ITEMS

- Invest in a discreet ID bracelet or locket that includes their name, phone number, and memory problem. If they won't wear it, have someone special give it to them as a gift.
- Engrave their name in such things as hearing aids, dentures, glasses, and keys.
- Attach a sensor to their ankle or wrist.
- Choose bright-colored clothing and mark it with sew-on or strong iron-on labels

inside. A permanent marker can be used, but make sure it's for fabric and doesn't wash out easily.

- Sew bicycle reflector tape on jacket sleeves.
- Experiment with footwear. Some only wander when wearing shoes. Keeping them in slippers may help. If not, make sure they have appropriate, safe footwear.

PHYSICAL ENVIRONMENT

- Keep the environment safe and familiar.
- Make changes in environment gradual, one at a time. Allow them to accept and adjust to it.
- Clearly label rooms with words or pictures. Put their name on their bedroom door. Put a picture of a toilet on the bathroom.
- Put furniture against walls. Remove obstacles in pathways.
- Decrease noise they may try to escape from, especially sudden startling noises.
- Use a recliner or rocking chair they can't get out of without help.
- Keep indicators of going places out of sight, e.g., coats, hats, purses. This is especially helpful with those people who won't be seen in public without them.

- Keep car keys out of sight. The car may need to be temporarily disabled. Lock the doors. Disconnect important wires. Remove the battery. These are some suggestions—just remember that a person who is familiar with cars will be able to remedy some of these "problems." The ultimate solution may be to move the car to another location or get rid of it completely.
- An intrusion burglar alarm will alert you to their attempts to leave.
- A recent move may increase wandering as they look for something familiar. Involve them in the selection process if possible.
- If there is a recent move, reassure them frequently that this is home now. It will take them awhile to understand that, if at all.
- If they recently moved, join them in their new environment. Slowly withdraw.

HANDLING DOORS AND WINDOWS

- A simple change in a door latch may be enough to stop them. Newer devices might not be familiar to them, like the bar or hook and eye latches are.
- Don't forget to secure windows.

Determined wanderers can slip out that way.

- Use a double bolt door lock but keep the key handy for emergencies.
- Consider electronic buzzers or infrared electronic eye alarms or chimes on doors.
- Camouflage doors with a screen or curtain.
- A "Stop" sign or "Do Not Enter" sign may stop them from going out a door.
- A single color for the bathroom door will make it stand out from the walls. Offer to take them to the bathroom on a regular schedule, usually every two hours during the day.
- A two-foot black painted threshold in front of a door may be perceived as a hole and a place to avoid.
- A simple bell or string of bells on the door will alert you they may be going out.
- Place locks out of the normal line of vision, either very high or very low.
- Use childproof doorknob covers.
- Put gates at dangerous stairwells; make sure they are high enough to stop a person, not trip them.
- Put fences or hedges around a patio or yard.
- Put locks on yard gates.

RELIEVING MENTAL STRESS

- Be aware that stress can increase or instigate wandering.
- Monitor their moods. Are they handling stress or trying to get away from it? Are they trying to escape unpleasant people? Crowding? Isolation? Are they looking for someone?
- Limit the number of people giving directions and assistance. One to one is optimal, though there may be times a second person is needed. One person should still be prominent, and the second following their lead. Two to one isn't fair, and will be perceived as overwhelming and threatening.
- Try to identify triggers. Are they trying to go someplace the same time each day, or repeatedly looking for something specific?
- Do they think it's a different time of day than what it is? Do they think it's time to pick the kids up from school? Time to go to work? This is one time when reality orientation, real or not, may help. "No, Lily, it's Saturday, you don't have to go to work today."
- If they are looking for something, help

them search for it. Learn their usual hiding places.

- Remind them that they are in the right place and you want them to stay here with you.
- Reassure them frequently that their family knows where they are and hasn't abandoned them.
- Reassure them that you're not going to leave them.
- Keep them busy and involved. Provide activities they can do for extended periods of time.
- Try to distract them with a meaningful activity if they are determined to go somewhere. If you can't, go with them. Follow them if necessary.
- Write reassuring notes if they can still read, and post them where they'll find them and can be referred to. Something like, "Betty will be home at 4" will help.
- Don't overreact or confront them about their behavior.
- Use humor and cajoling to increase their trust. Avoid telling complicated jokes that require the ability to remember the joke to get the punch line.
- Allow them to verbalize their feelings without arguing. This will relieve some of

the tension they feel and decrease their need to find a comfortable place.

- Avoid sentences phrased in the negative. Instead of "don't go outside," say "stay inside."

- Give truthful answers for loud noises. For instance, explain thunder. Avoid arguing or trying to convince them of a "safer" fanciful explanation.

- Keep familiar objects handy—stuffed animals on couches and chairs, a checkerboard on a table, the laundry in a basket to be folded.

PHYSICAL ACTIVITIES AND COMFORTS

- Monitor any medication changes. Some may cause restlessness, even if that isn't a listed side effect.

- Take them on rides in cars and buses in addition to keeping them physically active. If they get the opportunity to go out and see the world, they may not feel the need to wander alone.

- Develop a walking routine which they may follow due to its familiarity when they do wander.

- Allow them to move within a safe area.

Make shared exercise, such as walking, a part of the daily routine.

- While walking in a circle or in only a small area may seem dull to us, the physical activity is positive for them. They don't have the same need for variety we do.
- Watch for fidgeting behavior. Offer them activities to distract, keep them busy ,and burn energy. Simple tasks like sweeping, folding towels, doing dishes are comforting, familiar and can be done for long periods of time.
- Offer a massage for relaxation.
- Look in on them frequently. Look for signs of pain, fever, or hunger.
- Offer food and snacks frequently. Once they begin to wander, they burn calories. Give them finger food to carry around with them.
- Is the weather changing? Incoming storms with changes in barometric pressure sometimes cause a sense of restlessness.
- If they want to sleep in a chair in their day clothes at night, use your judgment. If it isn't harmful, let them do it.

NIGHT WANDERING

- If they wander around the house at night,

make sure rooms are well lit. Close curtains to shut out the darkness which may frighten them.

- If night wandering is a problem, limit after-dinner beverages, and always caffeine. Going to the bathroom may be what wakes them up and then they stay up.
- Limit daytime naps.
- Nightlights, signs, and familiar objects will help keep people in one place.
- Consider hiring someone to come in at night to allow daytime caregivers to sleep. Activities can be done at night as well.

L ou rubbed his eyes. He knew without looking in the mirror that they were red. He felt as if a week's worth of sand had collected in them.

He couldn't remember the last good night's sleep he'd gotten. Oddly enough, Rose wasn't doing anything new. She'd even been sleeping later in the mornings.

No, what kept him on edge were his own fears.

It had been nearly a week since Rose had wandered away at the mall. Since then, he'd read several of the articles and books he'd gotten a couple of months ago from the doctor. They all said wandering was an expected part of the disease.

But what sacred him even more was the point that once the behavior started, it would continue. That's what had his gut tied up in knots.

His cell phone rang, startling him as it vibrated in his pocket. It seldom rang even though he'd given it to the kids and posted it above the phone for Rose. He was surprised to see his home phone number displayed on the tiny screen. "Hello?"

"Lou? Is that you?"

"It's me, hon." He tried to keep the hesitance out of his voice. "What's up?"

"I'm planting my seedlings today."

"I thought I was going to help you with that this weekend."

"It needs done. I'm doing it now."

"Wait until this weekend. It's too cool today."

"It's not. I'm doing it now."

"Why did you call me, Rose?"

"I wanted to know where you are. You told me to call you when I have a problem." He had told her, then left her a note by the phone with his phone number weeks ago. They'd even practiced it.

"Yeah, you can call me any time."

"I need fertilizer."

"We'll get it tonight when I get home."

"Tonight?"

"Tonight."

"Okay. See you later." The phone went silent in his hand. His stomach that had been in knots grew tighter. He had a bad feeling about this.

After talking to his boss, he took the last couple of hours off. He knew from the look on Sam's face that this was turning into a problem. His nerves wound tighter as the fear of losing his job joined his other fears.

Driving home, he tried to call the house. No answer. Sweat broke out on his brow, and his heart beat loud in his chest.

He pulled into the drive and leapt from the truck. The front door was open. "Rose," he called as he stepped inside. No answer. He went through the main rooms looking for her. Then into the back yard.

Her gardening gloves and hoe were scattered beside the garden. He called for her. Still no answer.

His heart galloped now. His mind filled with frightening images and questions he couldn't answer. He raced back to the house.

Yanking the phone off the hook, he dialed his daughter's number. No answer. Then he called her cell. She answered on the fourth ring. "I haven't seen her or heard from her since this morning," Julie explained, the same level of panic in her voice. "I'll be right there."

Waiting for Julie to arrive took years off Lou's life. He filled the time calling neighbors to see if they'd seen Rose. No one had. He went through the house several times, calling her name, looking in every room. Even in the closets. He felt strange doing it, but he knew he had to look everywhere. He was just hanging up from calling her favorite nursery when Julie arrived. Nearly half an hour had passed, and he still had no idea where else to look.

Julie suggested they call the police. Lou resisted the idea, but he knew he had no other ideas and perhaps no other choice.

WHAT HAPPENS WHEN AN ALZHEIMER'S PATIENT IS missing?

You've looked throughout the house or facility for the person. But have you? Look *everywhere*. Even in places they don't usually go. Look under beds, in closets, under stairways. Don't dismiss a place just because they don't normally go there.

Search as if you don't know the person. Don't try to second-guess them. They aren't thinking rationally, but you'll try to think rationally. "Oh, he'd never go in there." Look anyway. You don't know what the person is thinking or imagining.

A search and rescue worker related a story of a boy who had been playing Superman. He'd donned one of his mother's blue blankets as his cape. Tired, he laid down on the blue sofa, wrapping himself up in the blanket. Family searched everywhere for him. Finally, exhausted, they called the police. The dogs came in and found him, sound asleep on the couch right in front of their eyes . . . camouflaged by the house itself.

Caregivers aren't trained in the level of observation skills that searchers are. Mix that in with worry and panic, and one's ability to be an effective searcher diminishes.

If you've search for a dementia patient for longer than fifteen minutes, it's time to consider calling in the professionals. An officer gives the suggestion to use common sense and trust your gut instincts. You know that feeling of knowing. You know they're gone, lost. That's when to call.

Often, people are hesitant to call, not wanting to bother anyone. "The police are too busy," is one comment frequently heard. Remember, it's their job to save lives, and finding a lost person is doing just that. After all, the patient may be physically hurt and need help. In interviews, they remind us that it's our tax dollars at work. Sometimes we need to cash in.

When it becomes a problem, police and rescue workers will let you know. Don't worry about it until then. And even if they've mentioned concerns in the past . . . still call. Deal with the need to make changes after the person is home safe and sound.

After you've made the call, an interviewer will arrive and talk with the family member or caregiver. They'll be asking for a description of the person. Height, weight, hair color, eye color, what clothes they were wearing. Where were they last seen? They'll ask for a current picture or video of the person.

Depending on the weather, manpower available, the length of time the person's been missing, and many other factors, a search will be launched.

In many cities, there is a program called 9-1-1 callback. The dispatcher's office will begin calling all the houses in a specific area with a message to alert the neighborhood of the situation, and give a few details for people to look for. Something like, "This is the police department. Someone is missing." Then they'll give a description with instructions to call 9-1-1 if they see this person.

If the weather's bad, if the person's been gone a long time, or there are any other risk factors, a larger search will be instigated. Many city police departments will have helicopters that will be alerted. The media will be notified and may broadcast information. Anything that will get the word out, and the eyes of the community looking, will be used.

The interviewer will not only ask about physical traits, but will try to learn as much as they can about the person and their behaviors. If they have a physical problem, such as weakness on one side, or have repetitive behavior, this may affect where they go. They are more likely to follow a curved line or walk in a circle if they are favoring one side for any physical reason. Repetitive behavior may make them follow the same path.

Searchers will need to know what level of dementia the person is at. Not just in order to design an appropriate search, but to know what to do when they find them. Alzheimer's patients are often unresponsive in a search. They don't answer when called, and they won't call for help. They seldom realize they are lost.

Once the team has interviewed the caregiver, and gathered every bit of information they can, they will set up an Incident Command System. This is a standardized procedure that emergency groups use, which describes roles and duties, and helps agencies and people who don't normally work together to become a cohesive unit. An Incident Commander will be identified and will direct the team. They'll oversee creating the tactics, monitoring the manpower, and planning how to use them. They will also track what's been done. They will grid the area using statistics and knowledge of the person and the area.

Statistically. 50% of lost Alzheimer's patients are found within half a mile from where they were last sighted. Ninety-six percent are found within 1.5 miles of where they were last sighted. The searchers will look in that area circumference first.

Most patients are found in bushes or natural barriers. When the wanderer reaches a natural barrier, such as a bush, a ditch, or stream, they can't figure out how to get around or over it. The search team will look in these areas first. They will look in areas that we may not consider significant, or that we might not consider a barrier. Again, their training in observation will give them an edge over a family member searching.

In rural areas, or where a wooded area is nearby, the officer may ask for a scent article. This will be of use to put the tracking dogs to work as soon as possible. An important thing to know is how to collect the scent article.

You will need an unscented zip or garbage bag. Turn it inside out over your hand, and use it to pick up the article. Don't touch it yourself or you will add your scent to the item.

If you've already been searching for the person and/or will continue to be a searcher, your scent will confuse the search dog.

Once you've grabbed the article, turn the bag right-side out over it and seal it. Hand that to the team member in charge of the search.

Take an item that has touched their body directly. Some ideas are sheets, bedding, underwear, socks, or a hat. Some of these may seem large, which is fine. The important part is that they have been in close contact with the missing person's skin. Choose things that have not been washed, and haven't been mingled with other people's clothing in something like a hamper. One very good item is the liner of a shoe. Take it out of the shoe, as the outside of the shoe has been everywhere and will carry a multitude of scents. Again, use the plastic to remove it. That scent will be what the dog is looking for.

There *are* different types of dogs. Search and Rescue uses three different kinds, depending upon availability as well as need. Tracking dogs will follow each and every footstep. Trailing dogs will follow the trail line, and air-sniffing dogs catch a scent on the breeze or wind. The air dogs can clear large areas quickly, while the other two types of dogs are more detailed; following trails that are even a few days old.

Police dogs, while taught to follow a trail, can only scent a trail that is around fifteen minutes old.

They are taught to search and detain at the end when they find someone. Search and Rescue dogs are taught to search and "lick you to death." The final outcome is very different.

Time is of the essence when searching for someone with dementia. They are often physically capable of walking long distances, but they don't have the reserves or the sense to care for themselves. Seldom are they dressed for outdoor weather. They are at a high risk for dehydration, and that plus hypothermia, are the two main things that can be dangerous to someone who is lost. Every time they breathe, when they sweat or urinate, they give off fluids. Without proper intake, they can become very dehydrated quickly, and that will only increase their confusion.

If a dementia patient is found within twenty-four hours, chances are they will be alive. Beyond that time frame, the statistic drops to only fifty-four percent. Waiting to call the professionals because you're embarrassed, or afraid they'll think you "lost" the person will only endanger them. Rescue teams don't mind being called en route and told the person was found. They'd much rather that happen, than reach the twenty-third hour of their search and find the person severely injured, or worse, knowing they weren't called in until many hours after the person disappeared.

After the team commander has set up the grid and the plan, they'll send out two types of teams. A

Hasty Team and a Canine Team. The Hasty Team will begin searching the "easy" areas. Following major roads, searching the house or building again, looking in the immediate vicinity. They'll be looking thoroughly, but quickly.

The Canine Team will be going out to wooded, rural and off-the-beaten-path areas before the search teams can lay down confusing trails for the dogs.

They will search in an organized, methodical manner. They've been trained in observation skills, in looking at things differently, in details. They have information for all types of lost people. Little kids and teens are very different from a frail elderly person. An important difference is that a person with dementia isn't trying to hide from them.

Searchers have information in field guides called "Lost Person Behavior Checklists" that are available to them. They'll take all this information and begin a specific type of search. Searchers caution, though, that this is only a guide. Lost victims don't read the field guides, so they can do unpredictable things. Especially if this is the first time they've been lost.

Statistically, seventy-two percent of wanderers are "repeat offenders." Once a dementia patient wanders, they will likely do it again. The first time they disappear, however, do not assume they will make that a repetitive behavior. If they have wandered before, let the team know that, and tell them about what happened before, where they went and where they were found. Any little piece of information can be of help. Do not leave out anything.

The team can benefit by knowing some of their habits, their likes and dislikes. What are they most likely to do? Give searchers a feel for the person they are searching for. It will help them not only in finding them, but in approaching them when they do find them.

Once the person has been found, the medical team will step in and examine them, looking especially for dehydration and hypothermia. Most teams have EMTs or doctors with them. The person's behavior when found will depend upon many things. What happened to them during their "trip", how long they were out, and their level of confusion. They can be easy to guide around, but we know what triggers can do, and that they may exhibit resistance and aggression.

Knowing the person well will help the team deal with them. Being able to get them to familiar surroundings and people quickly will also help. This may be complicated by their physical status, but familiar caregivers nearby can help. This may be difficult for a caregiver or family member who is distraught. This is a time to be calm. If a family member can't be calm, then it is advisable for them to stay on the fringes, and perhaps even stay away. The wanderer may not realize they've been lost, and your emotional reactions or over-reactions may escalate or cause negative or resistant behaviors.

Do not put them, yourself, or the search team at unnecessary risk. Let them be examined and taken care of before stepping in.

A search team will look for the person until they have exhausted every possible area and option. They will continue their search for as long as necessary.

There are occasions where a dementia patient will get into a car with someone. This can be a very frightening situation. It has happened that a person got into a car and gone from Colorado to California. The person went to visit a relative no one else knew about or remembered. Luckily, the relative still lived in the same house they had fifty years ago.

Check with relatives and friends, even if they are far away. They might not be there, but they could show up there in time. Look in places they used to live. Numerous facilities report that new admissions vanish and are found at or on their way to the place they just moved from. If they've lived in the same town all their lives, or for many years, their long-term memory will retain old travel paths. They'll follow those, finding in them the comfort of familiarity. While we're out looking for them, they might think they are on their way home from school or work. Old patterns are helpful to know.

Once again, be sure anyone with dementia is registered with the Safe Return Program through the Alzheimer's Association (see Appendix D).

Every day, new technology is being developed. There is new locator technology, but it is expensive and not readily useful or available. In time, that will change. Until then, we need to be as prepared as possible.

Having a dementia patient get lost and wander away while in your care is not a crime. It's nothing to be ashamed of, or embarrassed by. It's a common aspect of the disease, though not an absolute. Many people never wander away. It is, however, something to prepare for. Being prepared and never using the knowledge is better than needing it and trying to figure it out when you're sick with worry.

If the behavior is repeated numerous times, authorities may feel it is inappropriate for them to be in their current care situation. They can and will call in adult protective services if they feel someone is being endangered or mistreated.

If someone in your care wanders away frequently, that's a sign that perhaps it's time to get some help. Your options for that are discussed more in depth in future chapters.

WHAT TO DO IF THEY ARE MISSING

When a dementia patient disappears, generally they are looking to make sense of a world that is not longer predictable to them. Don't take their behavior personally. They aren't trying to get away from you. The following lists will help guide you through the process of looking for and finding the person.

HOW TO PREPARE AHEAD

- Keep a log. Is there a pattern of where they go?
- Keep an article of unwashed clothing in a plastic bag. Let search and rescue personnel know you have it. If you choose to do this, change it every month to keep the scent fresh.
- Keep a list of license plate numbers, make, model number, and color of cars they may have access to. Have it available for search crews and authorities.

FIRST STEPS TO TAKE

- Search the immediate vicinity thoroughly first—inside and outside. Look in unlikely places such as closets, under beds, and under foliage outside.
- Search risky areas. Review the environment for possible hazards such as fences and gates, bodies of water, swimming pools, dense foliage, tunnels, bus stops, steep stairways, high

balconies, and roadways with heavy traffic.

- Are there cars missing?
- Notify neighbors, friends, family, community groups, church, or clubs. Anyone they may have thought they were going to see, and who can help search.
- Notify local shopkeepers and stores of the person's disappearance.
- If you can't find the person after a reasonable search, no more than half an hour, call the police.

WHAT TO TELL POLICE/RESCUE WORKERS

- Know if they are right-handed or left-handed. They will generally follow the direction of a dominant hand. They will often go until they meet a natural barrier, such as a wall or fence and then turn.
- Think of all the possible places they could go or try to reach. Have those places searched first.
- Consider unique environmental risks in the community. What's nearby where they might go? Bus stops? Parks? Highway? Train station? Water? Rural risks are large open fields. Urban risks are cabs. Check these soon.

- Are there family members or friends they've talked about recently that live in other states or communities? Would they try to go to those people?
- Where was their childhood home? Are there old addresses from where they used to live that they might try to reach?
- Where have they wandered before? Check there.
- What was their occupation? Is there someplace they might think they are supposed to be? Where were they employed in the past? Did they go some place at a specific time? Where? What time?
- Did they have a strong hobby they might be trying to pursue?
- How readily do they accept and relate to strangers?
- Can they read or follow street and road signs?
- Do they have access to credit cards? Bank cards? Would they try to use them?
- Keep in mind the weather. Where might they seek shelter?
- Have someone stay at home by the phone and keep the line open as much as possible. For outgoing calls, use a cell phone or a neighbor's phone.

ONCE THEY ARE FOUND

- As soon as the person is found, it should be reported to the appropriate authorities, and other people who have been involved in the search.
- The following lists will guide you through the situation once they are found.
- Approach in a friendly manner. Smile.
- Approach from the front, your hands by your side, palms up. Make eye contact.
- Don't assume they recognize you. Say your name and call or ask his or her name. Gently look at or ask to see an ID.
- Act as if you're introducing yourself, extend your hand as if to shake hands. If they take it, gently shift the shake to a friendly hold. Let go if they pull away. Don't grab or push them.
- If they continue holding your hand, gently guide them back to where they are supposed to be. Act as if it's a casual walk and speak socially, friendly to them.
- Avoid telling them they *have* to come with you, and do not point out in any way that what they are doing is wrong.
- Use a calm, gentle voice.

ATTEND TO MEDICAL NEEDS FIRST

- The first thing a search crew will do—or you should do if you find them—is to check them out physically. They will ensure they are not injured, but if they are, that all their medical needs are seen to immediately.
- Pain and dehydration can increase confusion. Take care of the basic physical needs first. Then deal with the emotional pain.
- Offer them something to drink or eat. Do they need to use the restroom or need a jacket to warm up?

ATTEND TO THEIR MENTAL STATE

- Don't berate them, threaten them, or in any way try to intimidate them. Negative reinforcement is not effective as they don't have the ability to learn from their "mistakes."
- Don't let them out of your sight. They may keep moving. Offer to accompany them. Follow them.
- Ask them to come help you with something.

- If they want to continue in a wrong direction, make up simple excuses why you can't go with them and want them to stay with you. For instance, if the person is determined to cross a field, the rescuer could say, "But I'm not dressed for that." Patients have been known to follow the rescuer to a sidewalk, and back to safety.

- Walk with them and gently lead by stepping ahead of them. If they are going out one door, you can lead them around a building and into another door this way.

- Make conversation. Draw their attention to interesting things around them. "Look at that pretty house." They may realize they are in the wrong place and ask you to show them the way back home.

- Do or say silly things to break their concentration. Don't worry if they look at you if you're nuts. Better they wonder about you than wander away.

- Sing. Hum. These are fun, relaxing, non-threatening activities. You may be able to distract them into joining you in singing, and into physically coming with you.

- TLC is a powerful tool. Be generous with it.

CHAPTER 7
NOW WHAT?

Lou sat at the kitchen table, a cup of coffee growing cold at his elbow, and the newspaper spread out on the worn surface. He'd read the headline and first paragraph three times, and still didn't have a clue what the story was about. His concentration was shot.

He sat back and looked through the doorway to the living room where Rose sat in his recliner. A rerun of an old sitcom was on TV and she watched it, engrossed in the story.

She'd loved that show when it first came out years ago. Unfortunately, he wasn't sure if she knew she was watching a rerun or if she thought it was back then.

He'd learned to live with his curiosity and not ask. The times he had asked had done nothing but upset and confuse her. The resulting anger was too difficult, and today had been quiet enough that he didn't want to rock the boat.

Yesterday's panic returned in full force as he watched her. That was twice now that she'd wandered away. It was one of the behaviors he'd read about and one that scared him the most. What if he lost her? What if she left the relative safety of the house and was hurt, or worse, he never found her again?

They'd been lucky yesterday that the girl across the street who had come to stay with her saw her. They'd walked around the block and then came home, but not before Lou had called the police. They'd just started to set up a search team when Rose came home.

Suddenly, she laughed at the TV show, and he smiled at the sound. Sometimes, she seemed just like her old self.

He glanced back at the paper again, and his gaze landed on the community calendar. There was an announcement for a support group meeting for the families of Alzheimer's patients. He'd read about them in the literature the doctor had given him months ago.

He'd suggested to Rose that they go, but she'd gotten upset. She didn't like being told she had Alzheimer's, and refused to admit she was like "those people."

The volume on the TV grew, and he looked up to see her frowning at the screen. He'd seen her do that before. It was as if she thought she'd understand it better if it were louder. He frowned.

She might not realize she needed any help—but he knew *he* did.

He looked up at the clock. The meeting started in two hours. He was going, and he couldn't leave Rose alone, so she was going, too. He just wouldn't tell her where they were going.

A twinge of guilt nearly stopped him, but he consciously shook it off.

Early on, he'd read about "therapeutic fibbing." He'd resisted the notion at first, believing that the importance of honesty was the foundation of their relationship. But so was caring.

He wasn't lying to her to hide anything or spite her. She just couldn't handle the whole truth sometimes. Not because it was horrible, but because it was too complicated.

It was no different, he realized, than the times he didn't tell her about work problems, or the details of his talks with the kids, or even the tales they had both told to keep the Easter Bunny and Santa alive for their kids.

No, he wouldn't tell her where they were going today. They'd just go.

Half an hour later, Rose sat in the front seat of the car staring out the windshield. The fall had cooled the air and tinted the trees to yellow and red. "I'll miss my show," she complained.

"We'll be back in time," Lou explained knowing full well they wouldn't, and that she wouldn't remember if they weren't. He pulled into the parking lot of a small church where the meetings were held.

She read the sign on the door but didn't comment, just followed his lead. She stayed close to his side as they entered the room. About a dozen people mingled about. A younger woman with long brown hair approached. She smiled and greeted Rose first.

"Hello. I'm Theresa. I haven't met you before."

He watched Rose struggle, but her smile was polite. "I'm Rose." She didn't often add her last name any more.

"Hi, Rose. I'd like to introduce you to some people."

"Okay." Rose looked at Lou, and he was reminded of years past when he'd dropped kids off at the first day of school. He swallowed the lump in his throat. "I'll wait here," he reassured her, confidence in his voice at telling her the truth.

She and Theresa headed across the room to the other side of a partition wall. He couldn't see or hear her.

He tasted panic and nearly followed.

"First time." The woman's voice wasn't questioning, just kind. Lou turned to see who had spoken.

A tiny, older woman smiled up at him. Her short-cropped salt-and-pepper hair suggested more age than the blue eyes that greeted him.

"I'm Lydia Barnum," she introduced herself. "My

husband is back there. She'll be fine. Probably better than you."

He immediately liked Lydia, and within minutes, he'd met half a dozen others he liked as well. People who understood how he felt. Just knowing that eased the tightness around his heart. For the first time since Rose's diagnosis, he didn't feel alone.

For the next hour, he mainly listened, amazed at the varied group of people around him. All levels of society and types of people were represented. Every ethnic group. They all faced the same battle.

And if their stories were any indication, every level of dementia was represented, too. He realized Rose hadn't done half the things these other people had. And she'd done stuff they found surprising. As they talked, he realized they accepted him and Rose —behaviors, fears, and foibles included.

As he helped Rose into the car later, he knew they'd be back. He felt better and so did she.

Rose had done a simple painting project while he'd been talking to the others. When she showed it to him, the pride in her work surprised and pleased him.

She needed to feel important and part of something, he realized. And so did he.

Yes, they'd definitely be back. Especially if she started to exhibit some of those other behaviors. He knew he'd need their help and expertise.

BEHAVIORS ... WHAT TO DO

While wandering and catastrophic reactions are the most widely identified behaviors of dementia, they aren't the only ones. Just as each person is different, so are the behaviors they will experience, and the degree to which they occur.

With all behaviors, if handled wrong, they can result in a Catastrophic Reaction. Remembering that will go a long way to learning how to deal with any behaviors that occur.

None of these behaviors are abnormal for a dementia patient, but they may seem very abnormal to us. Understanding that it's the disease, not the person, causing these behaviors will help. It won't take away all the pain, frustration, and embarrassment, but it will help caregivers minimize the frequency and intensity of any incidents. And hopefully decrease drug use.

REPETITIVE SPEECH AND ACTIONS

Repetitive behaviors are some of the most frustrating behaviors for caregivers. The monotony alone will grate on the best of nerves. For the dementia patient, however, these are actions which are familiar, safe, and provide a sense of safety. It's comforting to them.

They may do the same thing over and over again because their brain is continuing to send the message to do it. Or they may remember how to do it, and they don't have to worry about failure. If the activity they are doing isn't harmful, let them do it. They'll eventually change their actions, or at least they'll be engaged in something that makes them feel comfortable.

Repetitive questions can be very difficult for caregivers to deal with. They've just answered a question five minutes earlier. It's difficult, but as a caregiver, you'll need to realize you'll have to answer questions a hundred times. You don't have to come up with a different answer each time. Our own need for variety demands that, not theirs. And they aren't trying to stump you, or test you. They are simple seeking an answer they can't remember. They aren't trying to frustrate you.

If they ask difficult questions, like where their mother is, or why they can't go home to take care of their babies, validation therapy is a good choice to use in this situation. Acknowledge their feelings, not necessarily their words.

"Where's my mother?" can be a painful question if mother has been dead for many years. Don't initiate the grief cycle all over again. It's okay to say, "I don't know. Why don't you tell me about her so if I see her, I'll know her." Or "She must be a wonderful person for you to want to be with her so." Let them reminisce. Ask them questions about their mother and what good things she did for them. Knowing their history is important, and if you can supply special memories, do so. Such as, "I've heard your mother makes a mean apple pie. Tell me about it." Or offer to make them an apple pie. Better yet, ask them to help you make one like their mom used to.

Distraction, as just described, is a useful tool in any behavior, but especially with the repetitive ones. Find a way to connect the thought or emotion they are expressing to an action you can carry out, such as making the pie. More than likely, the process of discussing the pie, or the shopping list for ingredients to make the pie, will distract them.

Don't just distract them, though. Listen to what they say, both verbally and nonverbally. Reminisce with them, but also be aware of what emotions they show about this person. Parents were often the ones who gave us a sense of security. Offer them that security. "You're safe here with me." "I'll take care of you." All these are reinforcing and comforting. A hug, offered and accepted, may be exactly what they need as well. The following are a few ideas to help deal with repetitive behaviors.

- Respond to the emotion instead of the question. They may want or need reassurance. Give it to them.
- Use a calm, patient voice. Don't indicate your frustration to them.
- Don't discuss plans with them until you're ready to do it. They'll worry about it and ask you a million questions about it before

it happens. Present it as a matter-of-fact, we're doing this now, event.

- Use simple reminders. If they keep asking when someone will be back, or what time dinner is, post a sign with the answer and direct them to the note. If you give them a time, be sure they can find a clock, or your next job will be to answer, "What time is it?" a hundred times.

- Use pictures to replace written instruction if necessary.

- If the behavior is a repetitive action instead of verbal, ignore it. Don't reinforce it, and it may stop. Also, if your frustration is growing, remaining silent will allow you to hide that frustration.

- If the fact that you ignore them upsets them, use another tactic, like distraction.

- Give them plenty of time to complete a complex task. They may need to do a step several times before they are comfortable doing the next step. Allow that.

- Gently touch their sleeve or arm to guide them to another activity or to break into their thought processes. It may jog them to do the next step of the task.

- Provide repetitive activities which will give them a sense of comfort and familiarity— folding towels; rhythm instruments, such as drums; sorting simple sewing notions,

laundry, or nuts and bolts; washing
tabletops; dusting; Or stirring.

The following list is of general guidelines for caregivers to help evaluate and/or prevent repetitive
behaviors.

- Remove items from the environment
  which trigger repetitive action. Getting to
  know the person will tell you what these
  things are.
- Report anything with a sudden onset to
  the doctor. Something's changing and they
  need to be aware of it.
- Repetitive motions, like sticking out their
  tongue, twitching muscles, or involuntary
  movements may be the side effects of
  medications, not the dementia. Contact
  the doctor if you aren't sure of this
  behavior.
- Keep a log of what triggers the behavior
  and what approaches worked to move
  them on. You won't always remember
  them later. Reading the log on occasion
  will remind you and help you learn new
  approaches as well. Also log what didn't
  work and why.
- If a person continues to repeat the same
  word, phrase or name over and over again,
  it may have special meaning. Talk to family

and friends and see if you can learn the meaning and tap into the emotion triggering it to stick in their mind.

- We all have limits. If you are at the end of your rope, call in reinforcements and take a break. Sometimes just ten or fifteen minutes of private time will ease the sense of frustration constant repetition can cause.

PACING AND WANDERING

Pacing is often associated with wandering, and may result in a person wandering away. It may not be related, however, and pacing in itself is usually a distinct behavior. The dementia patient will often walk back and forth in the same small area, turning or shifting direction when they reach a real or imagined obstacle.

Trying to stop a person from pacing will only increase their frustration, and will often result in a Catastrophic Reaction. There are other alternatives which will work to incorporate this person into the activities of the home or facility, and still accomplish what you need without an altercation.

There is a trigger for this type of behavior. Look for signs of what started the pacing. It is not necessary to solve the "problem" or stop them if the behavior is not endangering them or someone else. Incorporate the behavior into their normal routine. If you're doing a task, do a piece of it each time they pass by. If there's an activity or game going on, when they come past, it's their turn.

If you are trying to accomplish a task such as brushing teeth, let them brush as they walk. If it's meal time, hand them a different finger food as they pass. Constant wanderers and pacers burn lots of calories. They will often carry and eat food with them. Put things in hot dog buns, wraps or tortillas. On-the-go food will help.

If their safety is involved, and there are places they need to keep out of, lock them out. If that isn't possible, be creative in blocking their path. They will turn or stop at a barrier. Put a piece of furniture in their way, but make sure it's big enough for them to see, and not trip over.

Yellow ribbons at eye level will create a visual barrier. This has worked in facilities to keep residents out of each others' rooms and can easily be adapted to the home environment. A little Velcro and a length of thick yellow ribbon can be very useful.

Another option is to put a black strip of paint across the floor. The dementia patient will perceive this as a hole, or a step, and not cross it. Make it wide enough to be seen, at least a foot across.

And if you can't change the behavior, join them. You can walk and get dressed except for pants, shoes, and socks. You can eat on the run. About the only thing you can't do when you're in constant motion is sleep.

There will come a time when a constant wanderer will need to stop and rest, but their body just keeps on going. The following list gives suggestions for halting their pacing at times like this.

- Sit down with them on a comfortable couch, or lie down with them on a bed. Hold their hand, rub their back, or do other soothing motions.
- Soft music may slow them down.
- Aromatherapy is useful. Soft relaxing scents like lavender can soothe them.
- If they sit or stop someplace, leave them there. Don't try to move them to a chair or bed you think would be more comfortable. They'll just wake up and keep going.
- Give them something big to hold onto, like a large stuffed animal that isn't easily disposed of. They'll sit and hold it and not be able to use their hands to push up out of a chair.
- Beanbag chairs and recliners have been used for years as comfortable ways to stop a person from constantly moving. Don't leave them seated there for long, as they may try to get up and fall, or become frustrated at trying to rise and not being able to.
- Dance with them. The constant rhythm may ease their need to move, and slow

their pace enough to guide them to a sitting position.

- Provide a safe environment, or a room, where they can wander to their heart's content in safety. Provide visual stimulation along their path such as wall hangings they can touch, familiar photos, and special objects. Being in a comfortable, familiar place may ease their need to wander and move.

- Remove things from the environment which may indicate they need to get up and move. A coat rack, for example, is an indicator that people leave this place. Purses provide the same indication, and suitcases are a strong trigger that someone is leaving. Keep these out of sight.

PILLAGING AND HOARDING

Two behaviors that are linked are pillaging and hoarding. This is when the person takes things and hides them in secret places, even in clothing. They are looking for something familiar to cling to, something that's theirs. Having lost the ability to understand that everything isn't theirs, they may take other people's personal items. Having possessions is important to all of us. It says we're successful, important, and belong. The person is simply seeking that same feeling.

Listed below are suggestions of how to keep the environment safe.

- Keep dangerous items such as silverware, knives, and forks out of reach. Cut food for them so they don't need a knife, and provide plastic utensils as much as possible. (Note: cut the food before it's served to them; otherwise they'll feel demeaned to have their food cut like a child's in front of others.)

- Provide them objects they can keep and hide away. Keep small trinkets, such as soft scarves and costume jewelry in a dresser, desk drawer, or closet. On occasion, check rooms and return these items to the drawer, so they can rummage and "borrow" all over again.

- Keep other drawers and closets locked and secured.

- Old-fashioned locks, such as hook and eye locks, or slide bolts will long be remembered, and are easy to figure out through trial and error. Key locks or locks placed above eye level will work better. Use the same key for all the locks, so caregivers aren't carrying a huge chain of keys.

- Keep lots of things that are safe and familiar out in plain sight. Avoid valuable or breakable objects, but keep things out that they can pick up. If they have a special interest, keep numerous objects associated with that interest available. If they were a gardener, keep bulb magazines or books on gardens handy. With many around, they may not feel the need to keep the "one" for themselves.

Listed below are ways to retrieve or find missing items.

- Tug of war isn't a game you want to get in to. Just as with any argument, they don't know they can't win. Let them have it and just keep an eye out and pick it up when they set it down.
- Trade one item for another. It works with us all. Food works well, but so do stuffed animals, favorite objects, and the opportunity to hold hands with a real person.
- Avoid buying clothing with pockets. Less likelihood of them filling them.
- Check the pockets of their clothing before washing and the trash can before throwing it out. If they hoard, they will likely hide their hoard so no one will find it. Note where they hide things and if things come up missing, look in those places. Wait until

they get dressed for bed and remove the items when they aren't aware of it.

- Many people have gone hungry at some time in their life. Those memories and that fear may return. Let them have their hoard as security. Clean their room and hiding places regularly.

- If they hide food or try to take food with them when they leave the meal, keep finger foods always sitting out in plain view. Cookies, bananas, vegetables are all easily pocketed, and easily cleaned out later. Since they may think they are in a strange place, or won't remember where to get food if they are hungry, they'll be reassured if they can see it clearly.

- Check their room and hiding places when they are distracted elsewhere. Have a family member or friend visit so you can disappear for a few minutes. Don't search their room or personal space when they can see you, or try to sneak when there's a chance they'll walk in on you. Violating their trust will be a difficult thing to fix. They may not remember you or what you did, but the emotion of you doing something negative to them will remain.

DELUSIONS AND HALLUCINATIONS

Delusions are common in dementia patients. They are the set belief that something, which is incorrect or unreal, is true. Most delusions accompanying dementia are harmless. An example would be a person who thinks she is spending her day at a country club with friends. It isn't necessary for her to know she isn't at a club, or possibly even in a different state. This type of delusion is harmless, and destroying it can upset her.

Delusions that are upsetting, on the other hand, can be a problem. If the person believes they are in jail, or a concentration camp, they may need reassurance that the delusion is not true. Tread carefully when reorienting them. Reality Orientation is not appropriate. Reassuring them that they are not in a concentration camp, but are in America with you, and are safe, is important.

Hallucinations are things heard or seen by only that person. While to us, these may not exist, to them they are very real. Telling them otherwise is not appropriate. Neither is agreeing with them.

If she sees children in her bed, reassure her that you'll help her fix the bed and watch out for her. Don't agree that you see the children when you don't.

Sometimes something as simple as turning on the light, or adjusting the curtains, will make the hallucination go away. Distracting them with a soothing, comforting activity may help. Being there and reassuring them that you'll take care of them, and everything around them will go a long way to helping them.

Making sure there isn't a separate health reason for the delusions and hallucinations will help also. The following list is a checklist regarding their health.

- Have vision and hearing checked regularly. Provide appropriate glasses and hearing aids and keep them clean and in good repair.
- Check for illnesses, such as an infection or urinary tract infection (UTI) which can affect clear thought processes.
- Notify the doctor. Medications may help, or medications may need to be checked for any interactions, especially if they have recently begun taking something over the counter, such as cold medication.
- Check the person's skin when they are changing clothes or bathing. Are there bruises or marks that indicate they may have fallen and possibly bumped their head?
- Monitor their fluid intake. Make sure they are getting plenty to drink. Seniors, especially those with dementia, are prone to dehydration which will increase

confusion and their ability to interpret their environment.

- Adjust lighting. Diminish extra or strange noises. Changes or deficits in hearing and vision may make them interpret what they see and hear incorrectly.

DEALING WITH THE ENVIRONMENT AND ACCUSATIONS

- Change the environment as little as possible. Change will indicate chaos to them. They won't be able to adjust. If change is necessary, make it slowly, and incrementally. One step at a time.
- Investigate their concerns. They may actually be missing something, or had someone in their room who has now left. Don't automatically dismiss their claim because they have dementia.
- If they believe something has been stolen from them, take their concern seriously. Offer to help them search for it, let them tell you what they think happened, and acknowledge their feelings of loss and anger.

REMOVING CLOTHING

Removing clothing in a public setting is a definite taboo for society. For a dementia patient, it is more likely an attempt to get comfortable. They may be too hot, they may be wearing clothing they don't like or which is uncomfortable. For whatever reason, it is not a sexual behavior, nor should it be misinterpreted as such.

It also may be a sign that they need to go to the bathroom. They know their body is uncomfortable, from a full bladder in this case, but they can't cognitively identify the cause of their discomfort. So they begin to try and solve the problem.

They may think it's nine in the evening instead of nine in the morning and that it's time to get ready for bed. All they need to do now is find the bed to lie down on. For caregivers who've just spent an hour getting them dressed, this may be very frustrating.

The following list gives suggestions of how to handle this behavior.

- Offer to take them to the restroom frequently. Every two hours will usually hit most of the times their body is uncomfortable.
- Monitor their weight. If they are gaining or losing weight, their clothes won't fit properly.
- Did the person wear—or not wear—a

certain piece of clothing on a regular basis? Shoes are often an article of clothing people don't wear at home. The same with sweaters or heavy clothing like sweatshirts. They take them off out of habit.

- Buy easy-on, easy-off clothes. Yes, they will be able to take them off more easily, but you'll spend less time putting them back on as well.

- Clothing with simple, or no closures such as zippers and snaps which are distracting, may diminish the need to fidget and remove clothes.

- Removing such things as glasses, dentures, and hearing aids falls into the same category. Do they fit or work properly? Are they comfortable? If they continue to remove them, even with proper care and fitting, can they do without them? It may be upsetting to see someone without their glasses or teeth if they've always worn them, but if they are calmer, the trade-off is more important. We cognitive people can adjust. They can't.

INAPPROPRIATE OR EMBARRASSING BEHAVIOR

Dementia patients experience a loss of impulse control which can result in inappropriate behavior. The ability to control impulses is a response learned early in childhood, and will be erased by dementia. Many times, they are simply speaking aloud what we all think in our mind. They may not even be aware they've spoken.

In the past, the person would have been mortified by their own behavior, but dementia takes that ability from them. The disease is at fault, not them, and certainly not anyone else.

This is one behavior where distraction and keeping them busy is important. If they are focused on an activity, they won't be worrying about or noticing the world around them.

For example, if they often comment on how bad someone looks, avoid having that person around them. Or better yet, explain to the cognitive person about the disease and warn them to expect the behavior.

- Avoid situations where you know they'll be put in a position of having to keep their opinions to themselves, or be around people you know they'll vocalize something negative about.
- Don't be embarrassed by their behavior. You didn't cause it.
- Avoid apologizing for their behavior in front of them. Ignore the behavior, and don't draw attention to it. Explain later to people who may need to understand what's

happening. Otherwise, don't worry about it.

- Don't reprimand or argue with the person. That only increases their—and your —frustration

---

SLEEP DISTURBANCES

Sleep disturbances are common in seniors, and even more pronounced in dementia patients. As we age, we need less sleep, partially because we aren't as active, and sometimes because we nap during the day. Dementia patients often get their days and nights confused as well.

Sometimes, what we consider sleep disturbances, however, are actually lifelong patterns that don't match ours. Night owls and early birds can create conflicts when living together. Older adults only need six to eight hours of sleep, and it's somewhat baffling that people go to bed early and wonder why they wake up early. After going to bed at ten at night, it isn't unusual for a person to wake up at four in the morning and be ready to go. On the flipside, a person who stays up late isn't going to be able to get up early. Schedules need to follow the body's natural rhythm and habit.

Many nighttime behaviors are created by caregiver's behavior. That should be one of the first places we look when the question comes up about sleep disturbances. Adjust that behavior first, then look at other causes.

CHECK PHYSICAL NEEDS

- Ask the doctor to examine when diuretic medications are given. Having to get up to go to the bathroom several times at night can alter someone's sleep patterns.
- Sleep medications often have the opposite effect in a dementia patient. Use them only as a last resort.
- Make sure any pain is appropriately and adequately treated. Aches and pains can keep anyone awake.
- Make sure the person isn't too hot or too cold. That will wake someone and instigate their getting up. They may then forget why they got up and think it's time to get up for the day.
- Minimize or eliminate caffeine intake if possible. If they are long-time caffeine drinkers, slowly wean them off it as they will have some withdrawal. If caffeine in the morning helps wake them up, and establish the wake-up routine, it may be important to keep the routine but not at other times.

- Avoid or cut down alcohol intake. A single drink may be relaxing, especially if it's a life-long pattern. Be sure the doctor is aware of their intake, as there may be medications which shouldn't be taken if they are drinking alcohol.
- Make sure the person goes to the bathroom before going to bed.
- Make sure they aren't hungry and will get up to get a "midnight snack." Offer a comfort food snack before bed if they didn't eat a good dinner. Herbal teas and milk are often relaxing foods.
- Encourage adequate exercise. Using up energy during the day will help them sleep more soundly at night. Taking a walk early in the day or afternoon may help.
- Avoid exercise or physical activity late in the afternoon or evening. That will wake them up rather than wear them out to sleep.
- Avoid bathing late in the day or evening unless a warm bath relaxes them.

CHECK MENTAL NEEDS

- Determine if they were a night owl or an early bird throughout their life. Adjust the schedule to match theirs. They can't adjust. We need to.

- Keep them busy during the day and avoid letting them take a long nap. If they catnap in a chair, that may be better than an actual nap on a bed which indicates bedtime.

- Set or continue bedtime rituals—reading before bed, a glass of milk, music, putting on lotions or face creams. Offer a leg or back massage to relax them. Soothing scented lotions feel good and relax us.

- Avoid getting ready for the next day when they are going to bed. They may become confused and think they are getting up, not going to bed. Discuss today. Worry about tomorrow, tomorrow. Don't lay out tomorrow's clothes.

- Send "sleep" signals. Turn off the television. Turn down the lights. Close doors and window shades. Even if you aren't going to bed yet, set the scene that everyone is going to bed. No one likes to be left out, and they'll want to get up to see what's going on.

- Let them sleep in a recliner on the couch if they prefer and won't get into bed.

CHECK THE ENVIRONMENT

If a caregiver needs to sleep, consider hiring a night-time caregiver who will remain awake through the night. They can do tasks around the house if the dementia person sleeps, or monitor and interact with them if they are up. They don't have to continually try to get the person to go back to bed, though that will be the overall goal. While they are up and awake, they need to avoid activities which indicate it's time to get up, e.g., a loud television or cooking foods which are enticing.

- Make the house as safe as possible for them to roam at night. You may be asleep and not hear them. Lock all the doors, close all the cabinets, and remove any objects which may be dangerous.
- Make the bedroom familiar for them. Familiar bed, blankets, and pillows will help encourage a person to stay in bed. It's often the inclination to buy new things when you move to a new place, but that may be confusing and provide more stimuli to adjust to. Keep it familiar and make changes slowly.
- Use appropriate lighting, such as night lights, so that if they get up, they are safe in finding the bathroom. Also this will diminish shadows and confusion.

DEPRESSION

Depression is a condition which can be caused by dementia, and which can also increase dementia. It shouldn't be confused with the sadness or "blues" we all experience from time to time, or with the normal reactions we have to grief, loss, or just a downright bad day.

Depression is characterized by withdrawal, list-lessness, a sense of worthlessness, and disinterest in the world and people around us. It is a frequently undiagnosed condition in seniors, especially dementia patients.

Most dementia victims know something is wrong. They know they aren't in the place they think they should be, and that they aren't with the people they should be with. They definitely know they aren't doing things the way they have before. They may not know exactly what they've lost, or how things are supposed to be, but they know it should be different.

They also can't discuss their feelings due to their short attention span and loss of language skills. The cycle of depression and dementia can spin completely out of control.

Early in the disease, they may be able to acknowl-edge their losses, and they are grieving the loss of their own life. Comments by caregivers or others like, "oh, it's not that bad," or "things will get better, you'll see," shows disregard for their feelings. Acknowledge and allow them the freedom to experience their emotions. Offer support and reassurance. Be there for them. Let them cry if they need to.

Notify the doctor of their emotions, and any behaviors which indicate to you they are depressed. They may or may not treat it with an anti-depressant or other medication. The doctor does need to be aware of it, however they chooses to act.

It used to be a common concept that dementia patients couldn't benefit from therapy due to their short-term memory loss. That is no longer the belief, and certainly not the case. They can benefit from therapy, and their caregivers can certainly benefit from the knowledge gained about what is bothering them.

As people age, they often will begin a process called life review. This is a way of dealing with unresolved issues, and addressing situations that may have caused lifelong regrets. Dealing with these issues may be something the dementia patient needs to do, especially as they regress to the stage in their life where the situation was more acute.

It's okay to reminisce, to think and talk about life when it was better, or different. It's also therapeutic and healthy to talk about the negatives in our lives, especially if they are unresolved. As a caregiver, you can participate in this process. Showing interest in their lives shows interest in them as people, which feeds their self-esteem. It's also a way for families to gather an oral history. There's good and there's bad. If the reminiscing isn't comfortable for you, don't participate. If you need to, distract them or find something else to do. If necessary, talk to the doctor, or a psychologist who can be of more help.

Depression is a discussion for an entire book itself. The important thing to understand is that it occurs, it can be treated, and to notify the doctor if you suspect depression is affecting your loved one. Just because a person has dementia doesn't mean they have to suffer through something else left untreated.

SUNDOWNING

Sundowning in not an actual behavior, but the fact that behaviors predictably increase later in the day. Someone who is calm throughout the day will do things in the late afternoon or early evening they wouldn't otherwise do. More Catastrophic Reactions occur during this time, and wandering increases.

There are several reasons why this may occur, though nothing concrete has been found in research. It may be due to several things combined.

We all tire as the day wears on. Late afternoon is normally the end of our day, when things wind down. It's also a time of day when most people are changing their behavior and pace. They are getting home from work, starting to fix dinner, or preparing to go out to eat. It is usually a time when the number of people and events increases. No matter what its cause, it is stressful for everyone.

For a dementia patient, the day does not change in the same way. The cues that the day is winding down are there, but the change in actions isn't. They don't have a job to leave, new duties to begin. There's a sense of something missing.

This list gives some suggestions on how to deal with the end of the day and the occurrence of Sundowning.

- Avoid complicated tasks later in the day. Bathing, changing clothing, or errands, all should be done earlier in the day when they and you are fresh and awake.
- If medications are prescribed to be given late in the day, talk to the doctor about changing the time and dosage to avoid giving during this time. Giving medications at the noon meal can often head off late-afternoon behaviors.
- Sundowning also occurs when there are major weather changes, such as a thunderstorm, or incoming snowstorm. Family pets may also become more edgy. Plan soothing activities at this time.
- Light a lavender-scented candle or other calming aromatherapy scent. If the person

has a particular favorite, keep it handy for the tough times.

- Offer reassurances that you're there and they are safe with you.
- Allow them to be as free as possible in their movements. If they need to pace or wander around, let them, and provide a safe place for them to go.
- Plan breakfast and lunch as the bigger meals of the day and keep supper/dinner lighter. Finger foods they can take with them, or not have to struggle with utensils to eat, are best.
- Offer plenty of fluids to keep hydrated.
- Keep comforting, important objects where they can find them.
- Offer to show them or escort them to the bathroom.
- Make sure they stay warm or cool enough. Wind sometimes bothers people and will make them edgy. If they are outside, find a sheltered spot.
- If they need a catnap, let them, but don't let them fall asleep for a long nap on a bed. They—and you—will not sleep well in the night ahead.
- Offer herbal tea or comforting snacks. Avoid caffeine or alcoholic beverages, especially if they are already escalating their sundowning behaviors.

CHAPTER 8
IN YOUR OWN BACKYARD

Lou doffed his hat as he entered the neatly appointed office. The soft, muted colors helped relax him a little.

The sign beside the door informed him Meghan Reilly was the Admissions Director. A very young-looking woman smiled at him from behind the desk.

"Mr. Davis? Please have a seat." She came out from behind the desk and joined him at a round table near the door. He twisted his hat between his fingers before forcing himself to stop.

"I'm still not really sure this is what I should do." He swallowed the dryness in his throat. He wanted to bolt and run and go back home to Rose, but Rose wasn't there. Some other person inhabited Rose's body these days.

"Why don't I show you around? I'll give you our information, and then you and your family can discuss it?"

Lou relaxed a little more. He'd expected a hard sales pitch, but hadn't yet seen that. He hoped he didn't at all.

They left Meghan's office, and she showed him several parts of the large building. He saw the dining room, a large activities room, and a gym where he met three therapists. There was even a small room that was used as a beauty shop.

As they walked down the halls, Lou saw several rooms where people sat in chairs or laid on their beds. He saw sparse rooms as well as rooms that looked like mini apartments.

Finally, Meghan stopped outside two large, metal doors. "This is our Special Care Unit."

Lou felt his heart race in his chest and he took a couple of deep breaths. What was behind those cold, steel doors? The lock made a soft click sound, and Meghan pushed it open slowly.

"I always make sure no one's nearby when I open this door."

He wasn't sure if she was being careful not to hit them with the door or if she thought they might try to escape. *Probably both*, he thought.

The door closed behind them with another soft click. He looked back at it, and knew a fleeting sense of panic. He couldn't get out without help. Sweat trickled down his shirt collar.

"The rooms here are a little different." Meghan stopped at an open door and knocked. When no one answered, she led him inside. The room was sparse yet homey. He looked around, trying to see a bit of the person who lived here.

"Viola's family has done a wonderful job decorating her room. They like me to show it off." Meghan smiled at him, and he wondered if she saw the fear in his eyes. She gently touched his arm and pointed to a wall of pictures.

"We encourage pictures. These have been hung solid by our maintenance man."

She pushed on a frame, but it didn't move. It reminded Lou of hotel pictures. Meghan tapped the glass with her fingernail. "All the pictures have Plexiglas, and if you look closely, you can tell this is a color copy."

Lou leaned close but really couldn't tell. He did notice that a name had been typed and put onto the picture. "Tom 1963," it said.

"Tom was her husband." Meghan explained. Lou nodded. He knew just what picture of Rose he'd always want with him. Did she have a favorite of him? He'd have to see if he could find out. Just in case.

He turned away from the picture, and Meghan led him into the hall. As he walked by other rooms, he noticed that none of them were occupied as the others had been. When they turned the corner, he realized why. Several people sat on chairs in a circle. A young man was bouncing a big red balloon in the air, and they batted it back and forth to him.

"This is Josh, our activities aid. This room is the main activity room for the unit."

"Main?" Lou asked.

"Yes. We have two smaller ones so we can break into smaller groups without distractions. It's something special to the unit."

Meghan walked to a large poster on the wall. "This is our activities schedule."

Lou looked at the myriad of boxes on the poster. Several times a day, something new was listed.

"Art?" He looked at Meghan.

"Oh, yes." She smiled. "Just like when a blind person has more acute hearing, some dementia patients who lose speech can often communicate through drawing or painting."

"Really?"

They walked farther down the hall, and just a few doors down was a small dining room. The tables were set in even rows and much smaller than the ones he'd seen in the other dining room. Only four people could sit at these.

"We serve meals differently here on the unit. As you may have already realized, it's overwhelming for a dementia patient to have too many items to choose from. We only put one or two things on their plate at a time. We keep all the condiments off the table. It's a much calmer environment for them."

Lou didn't admit out loud that he hadn't really noticed that. He knew meals were a hassle, but he'd try that tonight. Just one item at a time.

A woman came in the doorway right behind them, and grabbed onto the edge of a table. She started trying to push the table, which was bolted solidly in place. Meghan walked slowly toward her.

"Verna?"

Meghan waited for the woman to look up at her, and then gently touched her arm. "Come walk with me." Meghan held out her hand, palm up, in an inviting gesture. Melody often used the same gesture with her daughter, Joy.

The woman let go of the table and took Meghan's hand. The frown that puckered the woman's face quickly slid away and she patted Meghan's hand like they were old friends. Lou watched Meghan gently rub Verna's hand in return.

They headed out the doorway and toward a desk that looked like it might be a nurse's station. "Verna likes butterflies, don't you, Verna?" Meghan told Lou as he fell into step beside them.

The woman's face lit up. "Flies. Flies," she said, waving her hand in an imitation of the graceful insect's wings taking to the air. Meghan walked up to the nurse's station, and a young woman stepped out and smiled at Verna.

"Let's go find your butterflies, Verna," the woman in blue said, and offered Verna her hand.

"This is our charge nurse, Nancy." Meghan made a quick introduction. The woman didn't look anything like any nurses Lou had seen in a hospital. Her clothing was a soft blue color with little designs on it. She wore sturdy tennis shoes.

Nancy led Verna toward the activity room, and

Lou watched them as they walked down the hall. The nurse listened, but even Lou couldn't understand what Verna was talking about. It sounded like mixed-up words, which it was. Still, Nancy nodded and smiled as if she understood everything.

Verna seemed so lost only moments ago in the dining room, a look he saw all too often in Rose's eyes. But a few soft words, a gentle touch directed to a familiar topic, erased it all in a matter of minutes.

Were there things Rose loved to do that he could distract her with? He thought of the garden she'd planted every year. Ideas formed in his mind.

Meghan led the way down the hall toward her office. This time when the locked door closed behind him, he breathed a sigh of relief. It hadn't been as bad as he'd expected, but still the closed-in feeling hadn't thrilled him.

"I'm amazed," he admitted to Meghan as he sat down at her office table. "You have so much patience."

"Thank you. I enjoy the dementia patients, but I have an advantage. I'm only here eight to ten hours each day. I can go home and relax. When was the last time you had a good night's sleep?" She handed him a cup of coffee and took one for herself.

Unfortunately, Lou recalled exactly when he'd slept the whole night through. Two months ago. Melody had forced him to come to her house while she stayed with Rose. He loved his daughter for it, but the exhaustion in her eyes the next morning made him feel guilty, and he hadn't let her talk him into it again.

"You've given me lots to think about," he said.

Meghan handed him a stack of papers, similar to the stack he'd gotten at the doctor's office all those months ago and every place they'd been in between.

"There's a list of some other options you might like to think about. Day care might be something you could try."

"Day care? Like for kids?"

"Similar." Meghan blew on her steaming coffee. "We do it here, and it's similar to the activity program you saw, except at the end of the day they go home with you."

"Oh." Lou nodded, deep in thought.

After finishing his coffee and wishing Meghan good-bye, Lou headed for his car. He sat there in the parking lot for a long time. It was a nice place. He liked Meghan and Nancy. They seemed to really care, and knew how to care for people like Rose.

His throat ached and he swallowed, not sure how to get the lump to go away. How come he couldn't learn ways to take care of Rose better? Maybe he could? Maybe he should? Maybe he shouldn't.

He started the car and pulled out onto the street before he completely lost it. This wasn't just his decision, though he already knew what he'd like to do. Now he had to talk to the kids.

Dinner was a quiet affair. Lou did what Meghan had talked about and only gave Rose one food item at a time. He also fixed finger food: chicken strips, carrots, and biscuits. Rose didn't get anxious and ate more than he'd seen her eat in weeks.

Melody had called the other kids earlier in the week and told them Lou would be visiting the nursing home today. They were coming by tonight to talk. As he cleared the dishes, Lou felt the dread creep up over him.

The kids were used to taking his advice. Now he needed theirs. It felt strange.

Wheel of Fortune came on right after dinner, and Rose loved to watch it. He set her up in her chair, and put on a pot of coffee. He had to make it when she wasn't around and then put the coffee maker away or she'd turn it on and burn the house down.

The first knock surprised him. He knew they'd planned to come over; he just wasn't quite ready yet.

Ryan arrived first. He'd driven down from the city, and had managed to beat the rush-hour traffic. Melody and Julie followed only a few moments later. They each served themselves a cup of coffee before sitting down at the table.

Lou sat where he could keep Rose and her chair in view. She stared at the TV, sometimes commenting to the people she saw there, but most of the time quietly sitting.

"Dad? How was it?" Ryan's voice was soft. He wasn't usually a loud talker, but this was quieter than normal.

Lou smiled at his son. "Not too bad. Not bad at

all." Lou pulled out the mountain of paperwork Meghan had given him. Then he described the place and the people he met.

"Well, Dad, what do you want to do?" Melody spoke first, her gaze meeting her sister's.

"I'm not sure I'm ready to put her there yet." Lou watched as all three of his children let out a collective sigh. They didn't want to either. He almost didn't have the heart to finish, but he did. "I do want to try putting her in the Day Care program."

Silence greeted his announcement. Julie reached over and took his hand. "Can you afford that?"

So that's what they were worried about.

"Maybe Melody and I could take turns coming over to watch her," Julie volunteered.

"And I could take some of the weekends," Ryan offered.

Lou shook his head. God, he had good kids. They loved Rose, and he hoped they loved him enough to be there for him someday. They were trying to be there for him now.

"Thanks. You kids are so good, but you have your lives. Rose wouldn't want you to give them up for her."

No one argued. They all knew it was the truth.

"Then, let's give it a try." Ryan smiled, though Lou saw that his eyes were left out of the matter. "It's better than what I thought we'd be deciding tonight."

"Yeah, me too," Julie said.

"Ryan!" Rose's voice came from the doorway and

they all turned to give her a smile. "Aren't you a little late getting home from school, young man?"

Ryan laughed. "Yeah, Ma. I guess I am. Can I have a hug?" She gladly took her little boy in her arms and Ryan let his head drop to her shoulder. "I love you, Ma."

"Of course you do," she teased. "You have to." They all laughed at the long-standing joke.

AGING ISN'T A DISEASE. IT'S THE FINAL STAGE OF our lives, not the beginning of the end. It can be a wonderful time despite the added risks and potential illnesses that come with the changes going on in our bodies.

In recent years, it's become common practice to begin thinking that our final years will be lived in some sort of facility. When physical or mental problems such as dementia enter the picture, that practice becomes more common and urgent.

It's not a law however, that anyone ever has to move anywhere. Placement is a traumatic event, and sometimes an unnecessary one. One of the premises of this book has been to teach caregivers how to deal with the behaviors that are a part of dementia, and which commonly cause premature placement. With better skills, our loved ones can stay home longer, and possibly throughout their entire life.

But should placement become a necessity, there are things to know about that process as well.

Numerous agencies such as AARP and the Area Agencies on Aging have booklets and lists of questions to ask when looking at a facility for yourself or a loved one. These are sometimes simple, sometimes complicated lists. One thing to remember, no matter which of these lists you choose to use, it is not what the questions are that is important, but what the answers are. Part of the reason there aren't standard answers given is because each person has individual wants, needs, and preferences. When you get one of these lists, sit down and take a few minutes to answer them. Ask your loved one who will be living there what they'd prefer, and consult with other involved family members. What does everyone expect?

You can't please everyone, but you can at least know what they expect. Then, as you examine facilities and services, see how many of their programs match what you must have. How many match part of what you need? Ultimately, there will need to be compromise, but the family members are the ones who decide what is negotiable. Stick to your guns. This may be the last place you or your loved one lives. If there is something you want, or need, make that clear and there will be a way to get it.

The big bump in the road at this point has to be, of course, financial. Any of us can have just about anything if we have enough money. Unfortunately, most people who are facing their later years are on fixed, and sometimes reduced, incomes. This isn't a time to be shy or secretive about how much money is available for care.

Seniors—and just about any of us—are reluctant to share our financial information with others. It's not common practice, nor prudent, but we need to find at least one person—a son, daughter, spouse, friend, financial advisor—someone besides the ill senior who knows the financial situation.

That financial advisor needs to know how much money is available, or not available, and take that into consideration as the search begins.

This doesn't necessarily mean, however, that you have to settle for less than you want. Even patients on Medicaid deserve, and can have, appropriate and good care in a nice, homelike environment. What is important is making sure the match is appropriate for the senior who has to live at the facility.

Additionally, after they are admitted, your "job" is far from over. Visit often. Remember all the questions you asked in the beginning? Keep those and make sure the answers remain the same. Things change, and can change rapidly. Staff changes, ownership changes, regulations change, roommates change. When this happens, are they acceptable to you and your loved one?

All these changes happen regularly, and your family member is always going to need someone to watch out for them, to be their advocate, and to speak up for them when they can't or won't. Not just to complain, but to compliment as well. The staff in facilities seldom hear the good about what they do. Just as in any other businesses, it is important to keep up staff morale. Family members and residents are key parts of that process. Anything to lower the high level of turnover in facilities is a worthy endeavor.

Your focus, however, is on your loved one and taking care of their needs. If you need to complain or make problems known, do so through appropriate channels. Don't let your concerns about staff, or perceived friendships with them, overshadow your obligation to your loved one. Likewise, don't let anyone intimidate or confuse you into keeping quiet.

Just as each facility is different, each state will offer different services and facilities. Also, each state will require different types of legal oversight to allow family members to make decisions. Check with your attorney and set up any specific documents ahead of time. It is often misunderstood that making out a will gives the person you've chosen as your executor a right to make decisions. They can do nothing until after you've passed away. You may need help, particularly if you or a loved one has a diagnosis of dementia, sooner.

And you may need help that isn't covered by your insurance or by government programs. Private pay is an option, and many times, the only option for getting something you want or need. Knowing what you want, and who provides it will help keep the costs down and expected.

The following lists give you an idea of the scope of choices out there. Knowing what is available ahead of time can help narrow your choices, steam line the decision making process and ease the stress of any transition.

LEGAL OVERSIGHT

A **power of attorney** allows someone to act in your place if you're unable to. They can't make decisions that would go against your wishes. We most often see these put in place to handle financial transactions.

A **medical power of attorney** allows someone to act in your place in regard to medical decisions. These two documents are distinctly different in what powers they give. They can be given to the same person, on the same piece of paper, but they are very different. Many people have a different person for each role. That choice is up to you and the people you want in this role.

Remember that whoever you ask to fill these roles needs to know you have done so, and they need to know what your wishes are. Communication is vital to making these documents and people work effectively for you. Make sure they have a copy of these documents.

A **living will** is a document that is not recognized in all states. It states your wishes when death is imminent or expected. It is essentially your last wishes. It doesn't give instructions to family members on what to do for other medical procedures if you are unable to tell them.

Do Not Resuscitate orders. Basically, if someone finds you, and your heart isn't beating, do you want them to use CPR (Cardio Pulmonary Resuscitation) to try and revive you? This is the actual order that tells people what to do. You or your medical power of attorney can make these directions. Again, check with your doctor and attorney to make sure it is done appropriately for *you* and your community.

A **guardian or conservator** is a person who has been appointed by the court system to act in your place. Their duties are specifically appointed, but may include financial and medical situations. This may or may not be someone who knows you and your wishes. A court proceeding is required for this person to be put in place.

An **elder law attorney** specializes in issues dealing with seniors. Many have focused training in laws and cases specific to seniors.

Adult Protective Services is a social services

program through the government which investigates situations that put seniors at risk.

The **Ombudsman** is a person who works through the Area Agency on Aging to help seniors who are in facilities. They help solve problems and oversee that care is being appropriately handled. Anyone can call the Ombudsman for advice or assistance.

SERVICES TO BRING INTO THE HOME

Skilled Home Health Care is that care which is provided by a certified professional. This service is limited and regulated by the Medicare system. This is a nurse, therapist, or other professional focused on rehabilitating the person to their new environment, making sure they are safe and appropriately cared for.

Medication management is one of the tasks a nurse can do for a senior. This involves setting up a reminder box for the senior or family to use on a daily basis. Nurses don't come into the home on a daily basis to administer medications. Family members can set these boxes up, but someone who is untrained should not.

Occupational Therapists are often misunder-stood. Their work deals with how we do tasks, not just on the job, but also in our home. They know the tools available to make life easier and can teach us how to use them.

Physical Therapists work with the actual physical movement of our bodies. They work on strengthening as well as getting and keeping our joints and muscles moving.

Speech Therapists should be called communication therapists. They work not only with how we talk to get our point across, but with the thought processes and problems that affect that communication and speech.

Mental Health Professionals are psychiatrists, psychologists, and counselors. Sometimes, clergy fills this role as well. They help deal with the emotional part of life. Depression and loss are common in our later years and can and should be treated just as well as physical ailments.

Non-Skilled Home Health Care is that assistance which is not necessarily medically based. These caregivers can do errands, cook meals, help a person with personal care such as bathing, and deal with the day-to-day chores. They can also be companions who bring activities into the home and take seniors out to enjoyable events.

Care Managers are professionals who oversee and

coordinate care for a senior. Often this is done in the home setting, but can be done in all levels of care. Care Managers are employees of the senior and are objective in their services. Their focus is on what's best for the senior. They can, and do, often stand in for a family member who is ill or out of state.

A **Geriatrician** is a physician who specializes in senior medical care. In nursing homes and assisted living, these doctors often come to the facility. There is a trend in some cities of these doctors going back to the old practice of house calls. With a dementia patient, this is a more successful way of providing care as it eliminates their need to understand a change in environment.

A **Gerontologist** is a person who has a degree in the study of aging. This is a broad-based degree focusing on all areas of life. Check for this credential for people who run services or provide services in the community.

DIFFERENT TYPES OF CARE FACILITIES

In **Independent or Retirement Living,** a senior lives in an area with other seniors. Often, this is an apartment building, housing development, or neighborhood. There are minimal services available, but it provides a setting for common ground. Staff may not be available all the time.

Assisted Living comes in two sizes. Large facilities are much like apartment buildings, but they offer services as part of the monthly rent. These services are usually things called Instrumental Activities of Daily Living (IADL) such as cooking meals, house-keeping, driving, those types of services that are external and can be done for you by someone else. Staff is available twenty-four hours a day.

The second type of assisted living is the smaller, group residence. They vary in size, but are usually located in a house and feel like you live in a home. These provide those IADLs and may assist with a few Activities of Daily Living (ADLs) which are those tasks we do for ourselves, such as bathing, dressing, using the bathroom. Staff is available twenty-four hours a day.

Nursing Homes, Care Centers, Custodial Care, Rest Homes—there are numerous terms for this level of care. This is a setting where a person who is dependent on IADLs and ADLs can receive that care. Staff is available twenty-four hours a day. There is a nurse on staff at all times.

Skilled Nursing Care is that level of care usually paid for by Medicare and insurance. This is similar to the skilled care in Home Health in that certain services provided by certified professionals is involved in the care. Staff is available twenty-four hours a day and a nurse is on staff at all times.

Secure Unit; Special Care Unit; Locked Unit. This is another type of care that has many names. Essentially, it is a part of a skilled or assisted living facility that is geared toward those residents who have dementia. The doors are locked, and usually have a key code for family and staff to use to leave. Residents can't leave on their own. Staff is available twenty-four hours a day.

Adult Day Care is not as widespread and is one of the newer entries into the field of elder care. This is a place that provides care, services and activities during the day while family members are at work or get errands done. At the end of the day, the senior goes home with their family. They may go the next morning, or only a few days a week. Some facilities have weekend service, but not all. Some are specific to Alzheimer's and dementia while others are for any senior needing help during the day. Staff is available only during operating hours of the center.

HOW DOES ALL THIS GET PAID FOR?

Medicare is like the health insurance you carried

when you were working. It pays for skilled care and those types of services you'd require in a hospital level of care.

Medicaid is the program which pays for a person's care who is indigent. A person who qualifies for this program has very limited assets.

A Spend Down is when a person has used most of their assets and is applying for Medicaid. They will be spending down the remainder of their assets in order to meet the guidelines. There are specific things that this money can be used for.

Long-Term Care Insurance is an insurance policy you yourself purchased previously to provide for your care. Each company and policy is different and the requirements to access it are different. A qualified agent should be able to explain to you exactly how your specific policy works. There has been a lot of change in this industry in the past few years.

Private Pay is where the money actually comes from the accounts of the person who is receiving the care, or family members who may contribute.

EPILOGUE

Lou stared through the grimy windshield of his car at the entry to the Day Care. He'd dropped Rose there this morning before going to work, just as he had for the past six months. In another hour, it would be the normal time to pick her up.

Today, however, he'd come early. The Activities Director had sent out special invitations. The facility was celebrating their anniversary. They'd planned a party with food, music, and a chance to meet some of the other residents and families.

He'd dreaded it all week.

Not that he didn't enjoy a good party. He and Rose had been to dozens in their life together. That was the problem. She wasn't Rose anymore.

She seldom talked, and when she did, it usually didn't make sense. He knew she recognized him, but she didn't call him by name very often.

A woman climbed out of a car a couple of rows

over. He recognized her as Lydia Barnum from the support group. She saw him and raised a hand. He smiled and climbed out of the car. It was easier to go in when he wasn't alone.

"Hello." She moved to his side, as if she, too, preferred to go inside with company.

"I'm glad you're here," he admitted.

"Oh, I wouldn't miss it. This place is a godsend. I want the staff to know how much I appreciate them." She lifted a plate of homemade cookies she carried.

Lou frowned. "Is that the only reason we're here?" That thought hurt.

"No, of course not," she hurried to reassure him, not meeting his gaze. Her steps slowed. "Maybe," she whispered.

A late model SUV came into the lot and Lou smiled, pleased to see his daughters' faces through the front window. They waved, and he and Lydia stopped to wait for them. Together, they all went inside.

The decorations were simple and elegant. Nothing that would be perceived as overwhelming by the day residents. There were twenty-five of them now, though they didn't all come every day like Rose. He knew Lydia's husband only came three times a week.

A small three-piece band was set up in one corner, playing softly. Lou recognized them. They came a couple of times a month to do music therapy and entertain the residents. A table sat in the next corner with a fancy cake, punch bowl, and other snacks.

The normal furniture had been pushed to the outer walls and the wood floor was open. It appeared there would be dancing.

He spotted Rose sitting in a row of chairs with several other women. She was smiling, and a warm flush tinged her cheeks. She was happy. She tapped her right foot to the music.

She'd always loved to dance. He smiled, remembering the high school dance where he'd first gotten up the nerve to approach her. He'd been seventeen. She'd barely turned sixteen. She'd been the prettiest thing he'd ever seen.

He wondered if she remembered. Her long-term memory was still pretty good.

The band picked up the beat just then. He recognized the song and thought perhaps she would, too.

Lou walked across that wooden floor. His heart picked up in pace, and he swallowed his apprehension. What if she didn't remember? All those seventeen-year-old fears returned—multiplied by fifty.

"Hello." He made sure to make eye contact with her.

"Hello." She smiled—that was a good sign.

"May I have this dance?"

She hesitated a minute, as if uncertain, then she nodded and stood. Her hand slipped easily into his.

When was the last time he'd held her? He couldn't recall. That hurt, but he refused to think about that right now. They moved easily to the music, just as they always had.

He saw the girls and Lydia watching them. They were smiling, and Julie gave him the thumbs-up sign. He just shook his head. Silly kids.

The song came to an end, but Rose didn't move away. He didn't either. She stood there an instant, her head against his shoulder. "Love you. Lou," she said softly.

His heart shifted just a bit. "I love you, too, Rose." He gently rubbed her back as the next song began, and they danced again.

He knew he was doing the right things for her. He wasn't perfect. He was trying to learn, but he knew he'd screw up again for sure. He had people to help him. He wasn't alone.

Things had changed in their life. She'd changed drastically, and he figured he had, too. The future didn't hold the promise it once had, but they shared a past and had the here and now. He'd take what he could for as long as possible.

That was the best he could do. And right now, that seemed like enough.

A GLOBAL DETERIORATION SCALE BY BARRY
REISBURG, MD

Level 1, No Memory Deficit

No memory deficit evident on clinical interview.

Level 2, Very Mild Cognitive Decline

Subject complains of memory deficit, most frequently in the following areas:

a) forgetting where one has placed familiar objects

b) forgetting names one formerly knew well

No objective evidence of memory deficit on clinical interview. No objective deficits in employment or social situations. Appropriate concern with respect to symptomatology.

Level 3, Mild Cognitive Decline

Earliest clear-cut deficits. Manifestations in more than one of the following areas:

a) patient may have gotten lost when traveling to an unfamiliar location

b) co-workers become aware of patient's relatively poor performance

c) word and name-finding deficit becomes evident to intimates

d) patient may read a passage or a book and retain relatively little material

e) patient may demonstrate decreased facility in remembering names upon introduction to new people

f) patient may have lost or misplaced an object of value

g) concentration deficit may be evident on clinical testing.

Objective evidence of memory deficit obtained only with an intensive interview. Decreased performance in demanding employment and social settings. Denial begins to become manifest in patient. Mild to moderate anxiety accompanies symptoms.

Level 4, Moderate Cognitive Decline

Clear-cut deficit on careful clinical interview. Deficit manifest in following areas:

a) decreased knowledge of current and recent events

b) may exhibit some deficit in memory of one's personal history

c) concentration deficit elicited on serial subtractions

d) decreased ability to travel, handle finances, etc.

Frequently no deficit in following areas:a) orientation to time and place

b) recognition of familiar person and faces

c) ability to travel to familiar locations

Inability to perform complex tasks. Denial is dominant defense mechanism. Flattening of affect and withdrawal from challenging situations frequently occur.

LEVEL 5, MODERATELY SEVERE DECLINE

Patient can no longer survive without some assistance. Patient is unable during interview to recall a major relevant aspect of their current lives, e.g., an address or telephone number of many years, the names of close family members (such as grandchildren), the name of the high school or college from which they graduated. Frequently some disorientation to time (date, day of week, season, etc.) or to place. An educated person may have difficulty counting back from 40 by 4s or from 20 by 2s. Persons at this stage retain knowledge of many major facts regarding themselves and others. They invariably know their own names and generally know their spouses' and children's names. They require no assistance with toileting and eating, but may have some difficulty choosing the proper clothing to wear.

LEVEL 6, SEVERE COGNITIVE DECLINE

May occasionally forget the name of the spouse upon whom they are entirely dependent for survival. Will be largely unaware of all recent events and experiences in their lives. Retain some knowledge of their past lives but this is very sketchy. Generally unaware of their surroundings, the years, the season, etc. May have difficulty counting from 10, both backward and, sometimes, forward. Will require some assistance with activities of daily living, e.g., may become incontinent, will require travel assistance, but occasionally will be able to travel to familiar location. Diurnal rhythm frequently disturbed. Almost always recall their own name. Frequently continue to be able to distinguish familiar from unfamiliar person in their environment. Personality and emotional changes occur. These are quite variable and include:

a) delusional behavior, e.g., patients may accuse their spouse of being an imposter, may talk to imaginary figures in the environment, or to their own reflection in the mirror

b) obsessive symptoms, e.g., person may continually repeat simple cleaning activities

c) anxiety symptoms, agitation, and even previously nonexistent violent behavior may occur

d) cognitive abulia, i.e., loss of willpower because an individual cannot carry a thought long enough to determine a purposeful course of action

LEVEL 7, VERY SEVERE COGNITIVE DECLINE

All verbal abilities are lost over the course of this stage. Frequently, there is no speech at all—only unintelligible utterances and rare emergence of seemingly forgotten words and phrases. Incontinent of urine, requires assistance toileting and feeding. Basic psychomotor skills, e.g., ability to walk, are lost with the progression of this stage. The brain appears to no longer be able to tell the body what to do. Generalized rigidity and developmental neurologic reflexes are frequently present.

APPENDIX B

FOLSTEIN MINI MENTAL STATE EXAMINATION (MMSE)

Developed by Marshal F. Folstein, MD;
Susan E. Folstein, MD and Paul R. McHugh, MD.
Originally presented in the Journal of Psychiatry,
December 1975.

You may give support and encouragement, and force a precise reply, but you should not give clues, verbal or nonverbal.

1. Orientation

What is today's date? (1)
What is the year? (1)
What is the month? (1)
What day is today? (1)
What season is it? (1)
What is the name of this place? (1)
What floor are we on? (1)
What is the name of a street nearby? (1)

What town or city are we in? (1)
What country are we in? (1)

Total Score 0 – 10 _____

2. Immediate Recall

Ask subject to repeat these words. Allow 1 second per word, and up to 6 trials. (*Score—how many recalled after the first try only.*)

Ball (1)
Flag (1)
Tree (1)

Number of trials needed to learn all 3: _____
Score 0 – 3 _____

3. Attention and Calculation

Begin with 100 and count backward by 7: *93, 86, 79, 72, 65*

Correct response = any reply that is 7 less than the previous number AND THEN spell the word "World" backwards (dlrow)

Score = the best of the two

Score 0 – 5 _____

4. Recall

Can you recall the words I said before?

Ball (1)
Flag (1)

Tree (1)

Score 0 – 3 _____

5. Language
What is this?
Watch (1)
Pen/Pencil (1)
Repeat after me, "No ifs, ands or buts." (1)
Must be fully correct first time.

Score 0 – 3 _____

6. Praxis
Take this paper in your hand, (1)
. . . fold it in half . . . (1)
. . . and put it on your knee. (1)
Avoid nonverbal cues

Score 0 – 3 _____

7. Language reading comprehension
Do as this says: "Close your eyes."
Should be printed, in capitals, on a separate piece of paper

Score 0 – 1 _____

8. Praxis
Write a sentence.

Any sentence, must include a verb and make sense.
Arguably, "Help!" is a satisfactory response.
Copy intersecting pentagons
Must draw 2x5-sided figures, with the central
diamond preserved.

Score 0 – 2 _____

Total Score 0 – 30 _____

APPENDIX C

Activities of Daily Living
Adult Protective Services
Area Agency on Aging
Assisted Living
Care Manager
Case Manager
Conservator
Continuum of Care
Gerontologist
Geriatrician
Guardian
Guardian ad Litem Hospice
Independent Living
Instrumental Activities of Daily Living
Locked Unit
Long-Term Care
Long-Term Care Insurance
Medicaid

Medicare
Medicare Supplement
Mini-Mental Status Exam
Neuro-Psych Evaluation
Non-Medical Home Health
Nursing Home
Occupational Therapy
Palliative Care
Physical Therapy
Retirement Center
Secure Unit (Care)
Social Security
Speech Therapy
Skilled Care
Skilled Home Care
Veterans Administration

APPENDIX D

WEBSITES

Safe Return Program

http://www.alz.org/care/dementia-medic-alert-safe-return.asp

The site where forms and information about the Alzheimer's Association's Safe Return program are located. Anyone diagnosed should be registered in this program. It's simple, easy, and provides an ID bracelet as well as a listing in the national database.

National Alzheimer's Association:

http://www.alz.org

The Alzheimer's Association is a voluntary health organization dedicated to finding preventions, treatments and, eventually, a cure for Alzheimer's dementia. Their mission is to eliminate Alzheimer's disease through the advancement of research and to enhance care and support for individuals, their families, and caregivers.

Alzheimer's Foundation of America:
http://www.alzfdn.org

A group whose mission is focused on the aspects of caring for Alzheimer's victims and their families.

American Association of Retired People (AARP)
http://www.aarp.org

An advocacy group that has information about all aspects of aging.

National Agency on Aging: http://www.n4a.org

To find your local Area Agency on Aging, enter your zip code in the search box.

Medicare: http://www.medicare.gov

At this website, search "Nursing Homes Compare." This will give you the information on state and federal agencies in regard to fourteen different quality measures related to inspections. This does not include facilities that don't accept Medicare/Medicaid dollars. Also note, this information is reported by the facilities themselves and should not replace the actual viewing of the state survey information available in all facilities.

Social Security: http://www.socialsecurity.gov

Information on benefits, programs and how to enroll in the various programs.

BOOKS

Finding the Words: A Communication Guide for Those Who Care
Harriet Hodgson; John Wiley & Sons, Inc, Publisher

Dancing on Quicksand: A Gift of Friendship in the Age of Alzheimer's
Marilyn Mitchell; Johnson Publishing Company

Talking to Alzheimer's: Simple Ways to Connect When You Visit with a Family Member or Friend
Claudia J. Strauss; New Harbinger Publications, Inc.

There's Still a Person in There: The Complete Guide to Treating and Coping with Alzheimer's
Michael Castleman, Dolores Gallagher-Thompson,

PhD, and Matthew Naythons, MD; The Berkeley Publishing Group

The Validation Breakthrough: Simple Techniques for Communicating with People with Alzheimer's-Type Dementia Naomi Feil, Vicki De Klerk-Rubin; Health Professions Press

V/F Validation: The Feil Method, How to Help Disoriented Old-Old Naomi Feil; Edward Feil Productions, Publisher

ABOUT THE AUTHOR

 Angel Smits received her degree in Gerontology from the University of Northern Colorado, but learned the most about the care of Alzheimer's and dementia patients through day-to-day contact with them and their families. First as a social worker, then in the role of director for multiple secure units in Colorado, she developed the skills she now shares through her lectures and writing. She is an award-winning author as well as the former co-owner of Care Decisions, LLC, a consulting, care management firm.

If this book really helped you, I would appreciate it if you would visit your book retailer online and leave a review. It really helps. Thanks!

Angel Smits
Colorado Springs, CO

How to contact Angel:

Website: http://www.angelsmits.com
Email: writeme@angelsmits.com
Facebook: AngelSmitsAuthor
Twitter: @angelwrite

Made in the USA
San Bernardino, CA
16 April 2018